POCKET
GARDENS

POCKET GARDENS

BY JAMES GRAYSON TRULOVE

AN HBI BOOK
WILLIAM MORROW AND COMPANY, INC.
NEW YORK

Half-Title Page Photograph: Mark Schwartz

Title Page Photograph: Betsy Pinover Schiff

It is the policy of WilliamMorrow and Company, Inc., and its imprints and affiliates, recognizing the importance of preserving what has been written, to print the books we publish on acid-free paper, and we exert our best efforts to that end.

Library of Congress Cataloging-in-Publication Data

Pocket gardens: big ideas for small spaces/by James Grayson Trulove

p.cm.

ISBN 0-688-16830-2

1. Gardens. 2. Landscape architecture.

I.Title.

SB473.T78 2000 99-43601

635.9–dc21 CIP

Manufactured in China

First printing, 2000

1 2 3 4 5 6 7 8 9/03 02 01 00

www.williammorrow.com

CONTENTS

FOREWORD

Outdoor space is an increasingly precious commodity. More and more housing developments, office parks, shopping centers, and highway construction sites gobble up everything from large open spaces to old, tree-lined neighborhoods. Private, outdoor residential spaces are perhaps the most vulnerable as larger single family homes occupy smaller lots and ubiquitous townhouse developments deliver postage-stamp sized gardens to their new owners or tenants. Urban dwellers, long accustomed to such space deprivation, now have company in the suburbs.

In some ways, this might be viewed as a blessing and an opportunity. Few people have the luxury of sufficient time or money to maintain large gardens or carefully manicured lawns. Many prefer smaller, more intimate spaces. Some who could afford to do otherwise instead reduce large open spaces into several smaller pocket gardens, each with a distinct function. Properly done, these gardens can successfully blur the distinction between the interior and exterior of the house and expand living space dramatically.

The projects presented in this book–by professional landscape architects and landscape designers–view these space-restricted environments as opportunities to create gardens that are both visually stunning and highly functional. Through careful and thoughtful design, these gardens can fulfill the requirements of the most demanding clients and complex programs. Many small gardens have just one function such as an intimate dining space or outdoor shower. Others have multiple uses, from outdoor recreation and entertaining to providing a spot for quiet contemplation. All employ an astounding array of materials and design features that offer big ideas for transforming a small plot into a grand outdoor space.

When confronted with small outdoor spaces, landscape architects often create multifunctional "rooms". For their own garden (*Courtyard Dining*), landscape architects Kristina Floor and Christopher Brown designed a series of interconnected patios beside the house. Each functions according to the purpose of its adjacent interior room. There is a dining patio off the kitchen and the master bath opens onto an outdoor shower room. Taking a different design approach, Stephen Stimson and Jill Neubauer (*Bungalow Garden*) used hedges, board fences, vine scrims, and tree rows to transform a narrow lot into small outdoor rooms for play, rest, and work.

Prized for its reflective qualities and gentle sounds, water plays a key role in many gardens in this book. Samuel Williamson (*South-Facing Terrace* and *Parallel Paths*) uses runnels to connect the garden to the house. Oehme, van Sweden (*Fountain Dreams*) employ a custom-designed granite fountain to create a focal point midway in a long, narrow townhouse garden. A broad sheet of smooth or cascading water can add depth and sound to a garden. Sheela Lampietti (*Carpet of Moss*) collaborated in the design of a water wall adjoining a terrace. The wall is constructed of wood-fired tiles and angled out at the bottom to slow the flow of water from the top. The thin sheet of water falling over the tiles visually animates a

Right: A shade garden designed by Dunn Hamelin Kane.
Photo by Charles Mayer

quiet corner of the garden and adds a pleasing murmur. For *Inner Courtyards* Ron Herman created a rimless pool at one end of an enclosed rectangular courtyard. Water spills over the edge in a perfect reflective sheet. When observed from the living room the sheer sheet of water adds sparkle and depth to the view. Water is also a dominant feature in *Hilltop Cottage* where two fishponds serve to anchor the garden.

A large pool may dominate a small site, but a swimming pool or lap pool can be accommodated in a relatively small garden. Samuel Williamson (*Pool Garden*) encountered an existing swimming pool occupying the major portion of a tight 30-by-37-foot site surrounded by low stone walls. Through the judicious use of color-coordinated paving and plantings, he successfully integrated this large pool into the remaining garden area. Landscape architect Raymond Jungles gave his pool (*Tropical Retreat*) the look of a lagoon by painting its surface with gray Diamond Brite. Artist Debra Yates added a colorful fountain/mural. In each case, the swimming pool was transformed into a major design feature within the garden. Oehme, van Sweden (*Diagonal Lines*) took the opposite approach to handling a lap pool by completely concealing it from view. The landscape architects placed the pool to one side of the garden and screened it with a grove of river birch trees.

Enticing outdoor showers for bathing can add the theme of water to a garden. In most cases, these are placed next

Left: A garden by Stephen Stimson and Jill Neubauer is divided into rooms.
Photo by Ed Levy
Right: Lush plantings shade an outdoor dining area in a garden designed by Mario Schjetnan.
Photo by Gabriel Figueroa

to the main house and are accessible from an indoor bathroom. One exception is an outdoor shower designed by Mia Lehrer (*Garden Spaces*). It stands apart from the house and is reached via a stone path. The design of the shower is unusual; it is framed by vine-covered wire mesh walls and resembles a piece of organic sculpture on the lawn. Plants also play an important role in the outdoor shower created by Floor & Associates (*Garden Showers*). Adjacent to the master bath, the shower is lushly planted with moisture tolerant plants including peppermint and spearmint, which grow between the pavers. They release refreshing fragrances when brushed against while showering.

Nowhere is space more limited and gardens more prized than in Japan so it is not surprising that Japanese garden design techniques often appear in small gardens elsewhere. Ron Herman, who studied landscape design in Japan for many years, was inspired by a Zen temple garden in Kyoto when he created the checkerboard pattern of moss and stone for *Inner Courtyards*. There is a Japanese spirit to Fountain Dreams where a dry stream of rock is imbedded into a terrace. For the small urban garden featured in *Carpet of Moss,* the designers used a spare and carefully controlled pallet of plants, stones, water, and ornaments to evoke the spirit and esthetics of a traditional Japanese garden while adding a few western twists. Pamela Burton freely admits that the Japanese *tsuboniwa*, or "jar garden" inspired her design for *Back Garden*.

While an intimate, secluded feeling is cherished in many small gardens, the visual scale of others is dramatically enlarged beyond their physical boundaries through the use of the ancient Japanese gardening technique *shakkei*, or borrowed view. In this approach, a distant view or landscape is incorporated into the design of the immediate garden. A spectacular example of *shakkei* is the garden designed by Mia Lehrer (*Borrowed View*) where views of Los Angeles and canyons are integrated into the design of a small hillside garden. Plants were carefully chosen to frame and punctuate these vistas including two stately palms that frame a view of the city. More modestly, the landscape architects for *Diagonal Lines* used low plantings at the rear of the garden to take advantage of views of a public park adjacent to the property.

The correct choice of plants is essential for any well-designed garden, particularly for a small one. Planting space is tight, and often the planting palette is limited. These gardens are often in shade, placing additional limits on plant choices. Charles Warren (*Garden Architecture*) restricted his plant pallet to hosta and varieties of ivy in the sun-restricted subterranean garden he designed for a New York City townhouse. In sunny Key West, Florida, (*Tropical Retreat*) shade is in short supply so the landscape architect used a dense and varied selection of plants to provide ample shade, texture, and color.

Issues of sustainability and low maintenance are just as important in small gardens as large ones and sensitivity to ecological concerns drives many landscape architects' designs. In locations where water is scarce, it is essential to use drought tolerant plants. The Mexican landscape architect Mario Schjetnan (*Sustainable Garden*) designed his own garden in a drought-prone region southwest of Mexico City so that gray water from the house is recycled back into the garden through a sand filter. In addition, pavers in the central patio are set on mud to filter rainwater that is then recycled into the garden as needed.

The ecology of drainage was integral to the garden designed by Joseph Volpe (*Drainage as Garden Art*). Directing storm water from the street and front of the house down the steeply sloped garden at the rear was both an engineering and design challenge. The water is ultimately retained in a gravel cavity beneath the surface of the garden and used for irrigation.

Recycled materials such as glass and concrete are now prime candidates for reuse in the garden, as seen in the gardens designed by Andrew Cao (*The Glass Garden*), Mia Lehrer (*Ground Cover*), and Susan Raymond (*Soothing Spot*). Cao hauled 45 tons of 5 different colors of recycled glass into his garden to create a place of memories of a childhood spent in Vietnam. Lehrer used recycled green bottle glass to build a terrace in her own highly stylized and unorthodox garden. The glass has been tumbled smooth enough to walk on barefoot. Raymond found that broken pieces of concrete from her driveway made excellent pavers for a small patio. The chunks of concrete are

interplanted with dichondra, a low growing groundcover which softens the edges of the concrete. Seen from above, the patio resembles an abstract painting.

The inspiration for this book and the basis for its title, *Pocket Gardens*, is Paley Park in New York City designed by the landscape architect Robert Zion. This tiny park, wedged among skyscrapers in a tight space on East 53rd Street, was the first of its kind, complete with chairs, tables, trees, and a waterfall. Zion introduced the concept of the "vest-pocket park", a garden where much of the ambiance of a far larger park is condensed into a pocket-sized space to make it a welcoming respite from the noisy, crowded city.

As this book illustrates, many landscape architects and designers are stimulated by the challenge of creating equally vibrant gardens in tight residential settings. Many of the projects that follow are the designers' own personal gardens and they often serve as laboratories enabling them to experiment with new plants, hardscape, and new design techniques. All of the gardens chosen for *Pocket Gardens* offer cutting edge ideas on ways to transform small outdoor spaces into lush, inspiring gardens.

James Grayson Trulove

Left: The entrance garden to landscape architect Pamela Burton's studio. Photo by Jack Coyier

Above: An outdoor shower in a garden designed by Floor & Associates. Photo by Christopher Brown

BUNGALOW GARDEN

Stephen Stimson & Jill Neubauer

When this property was purchased, it consisted of a small bungalow divided into many rooms and an undistinguished yard overgrown with knotweed, briars, and vines. In the house, walls were removed to produce fewer, more spacious rooms. In the garden, the site was cleared and regraded in preparation for the construction of the landscape.

Perennial and vegetable beds in the back-yard are enclosed by a circular fence. Mirrors mounted on the fence posts reflect the sky. For winter holidays, a single strand of white lights are strung at the top of the fence. The portion of the garden adjacent to the dining room features an oversized copper birdbath and a hedge of pleached crab apples, which separates this area from the play lawn at the rear of the property. Birches were planted in a crushed stone bed along one edge of the property while on the other side, existing dense vegetation was selectively pruned to create a hidden garden.

BIG IDEA:

The strong geometry overlaid on the site organizes the landscape into outdoor rooms for gardening, play, and rest. To create these rooms, the narrow lot was structured with hedges, board fences, vine scrims, and rows of trees.

Above: A large copper birdbath is framed by iris and wisteria.

Right: Mirrors mounted on the circular fence poles catch light and reflect the sky. Privet hedges divide the working garden from the play lawn.

Photography: Ed Levy

GARDEN PLAN

Right: A grass path defined by perennial borders of irises day-lilies, and astilbe bisects the circular vine scrim and leads into the garden.

Left: In the front of the house, a privet hedge was planted to screen the street. It is distinguished by the wave form clipped along its top.

Above: The clarity of the garden structure is revealed in the winter.

BACK GARDEN

Pamela Burton & Company

Above: A photo collage of the garden. Photograph: David Fletcher

Right: The garden is only 7 feet wide but it serves as a fertile testing ground for products, plants, and the landscape architect's ideas.

Photography: Jack Coyier

This miniscule, linear garden serves as the entrance to the landscape architect's studio. A California sycamore tree, planted only five years ago, has developed a wide canopy for shade. At the sunny end of the garden, a large urn holds water and duckweed; a Joseph's coat climbing rose adds textural diversity. This is a passion garden with intense color provided by *Callistemon viminallis* "Little John", red penstemon, and pomegranate (which to the Greeks symbolized friendship). Next to a wooden bench is a brick carved sphere called *Chaucer's World*. It was designed by Pamela Burton and artist, Ali Acerol. The garden serves as a testing area for plants, tiles, paving, urns, benches, and rock samples used on other projects.

BIG IDEA: The landscape architect looked to the Japanese jar garden *Tsuboniwa*, as inspiration for this project. Such gardens are so small that they might consist of one or two plants and a tiny water basin. Their most important function is to not only give the inhabitants light and air but to also provide space for little demons which dwell under the eaves of the house. According to myth, these household deities remain quiet if the garden is well tended. An untended garden invites tension and discord to the house. According to Burton, "Our *Tsuboniwa* keeps all the demons at my office happy...tensions are kept low, and we have a place to sit outside either in the sun or the shade."

GARDEN PLAN

DRAWING BY TOM GIBSON

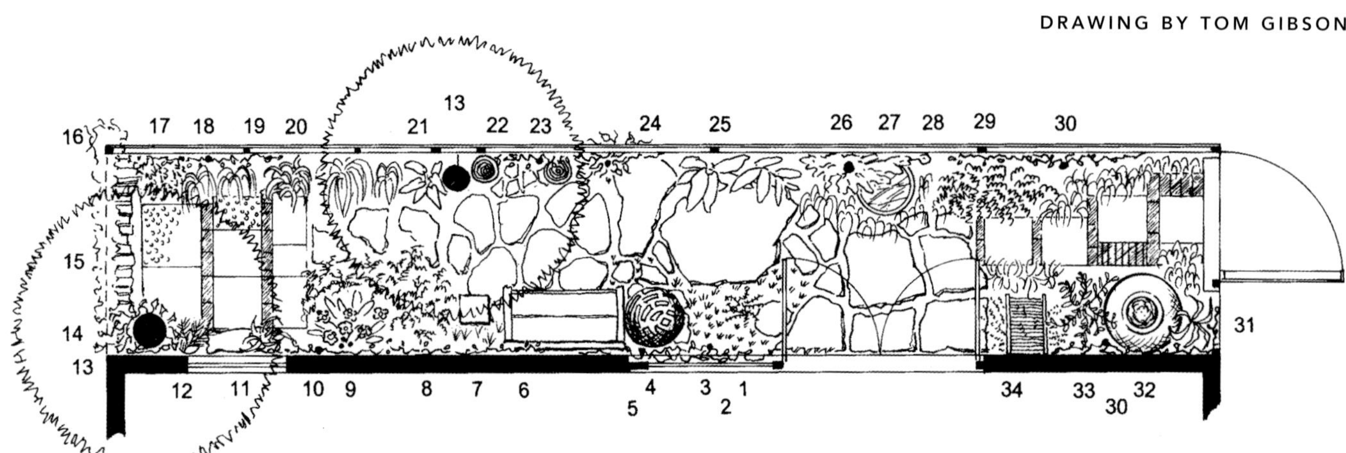

1	Acacia dealbata
2	Zoysia tenuifolia
3	Rosa 'Wife of Bath'
4	Gelsemium sempervirons
5	Ali Acerol sculpture
6	Bench and table
7	Carex pansa
8	Polystichum polyblepharum
9	Brugmansia 'Charles Grimaldi'
10	Rosa 'Golden Showers'
11	Bench with potted phalaenopsis
12	Rhaphis humilis
13	Platanus acerifolia
14	Distictus buccinatoria
15	Woodpile
16	Bougainvillea 'James Walker'
17	Ilex aquifolium 'Silver Star'
18	Pandorea jasminoides
19	Aristea ecklonii
20	Aloe aristata - potted
21	Zantedeschia aethiopica
22	Palm stump seats
23	Rosa 'Sombreuil'
24	Wisteria sinensis
25	Alpinia zerumbet
26	Punica granatum
27	Birdbath
28	Carex tumulicola
29	Callistemon citrinus 'Little John'
30	Rosa 'Joseph's coat'
31	Penisetum rubrum 'Burgundy Giant'
32	Water Urn
33	Pennisetum purpureum
34	Melaleuca eliptica at ladder

Right, clockwise from top left: The shady end of the garden; the bench provides a quiet spot for contemplating the day's work; a young California sycamore provides a canopy of shade; and a Joseph's coat climbing rose adds color to this passion garden.

SHADE GARDEN

Dunn Hamelin Kane

As part of the renovation of the house, this shade garden solved a number of functional and aesthetic problems. An existing walk-out basement required a creative approach in mitigating the extreme grade change along the house's west facade. By constructing an intermediate level five feet below the main floor and four feet above the basement floor, the landscape architects created a wonderfully soothing retreat.

Defined by the house on the east, a new stone retaining wall to the north, and a hillside to the south, the garden has a strong sense of enclosure. A 3-foot wide set of bluestone steps project into the garden and help define one of the planting beds. Offset access points lead into the garden from each of the four sides.

A variety of shade-tolerant, native ground covers and shrubs were planted in the beds surrounding the terrace. The plants help soften and minimize the five-foot high wall and provide a variety of exquisite textures and seasonal interests.

BIG IDEA:

The small fountain was designed to be the focal point of the garden as well as a hub to organize and resolve the different paths entering the garden from its four sides. The fountain is a simple, precast concrete box with an open top. A small hole was drilled into the side to run a waterproof electric power line to a small bubbler. Water is periodically added with a nearby garden hose. The fountain is an inexpensive way of adding visual interest and a soothing sound to this shade garden.

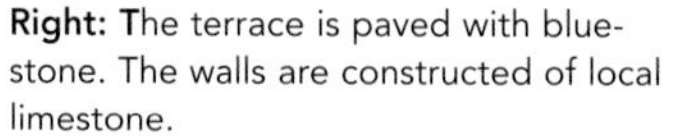

Right: The terrace is paved with bluestone. The walls are constructed of local limestone.

Photography: Charles Mayer

Left: A small bench of thick bluestone was placed across from the fountain and aligns with the steps.

GARDEN PLAN

LAWN
REFLECTING POOL
GARDEN TERRACE
FORMAL TERRACE
WEST LAWN

WRITER'S GARDEN

Dunn Hamelin Kane

The design for the garden of this writer's studio addressed a number of complex and often conflicting program goals. The owner wanted a secluded studio that was in close proximity to the existing house with minimal disruption to the wooded site on which it was to be built. For the building itself, the owner wanted a design with simple yet bold architectural forms that fit comfortably on the site. Through careful placement of the studio, the landscape architect was able to incorporate views of a distant mountain into the garden's plan.

BIG IDEA:

The studio was envisioned as an abandoned potting shed that had been restored. The central stone entry court is aligned with a framed view of a distant mountain and is flanked on each side with wide stone steps that lead to a loggia terrace on one side and the studio on the other.

Above: Detail of the stone entry court.

Right: Placed on the crest of a knoll, the studio is engulfed by native plantings that provide a sense of seclusion even though it is located less than fifty yards from the main house.

Photography: Charles Mayer

Left: A stone path leads from the main house to the writer's studio.

GARDEN PLAN

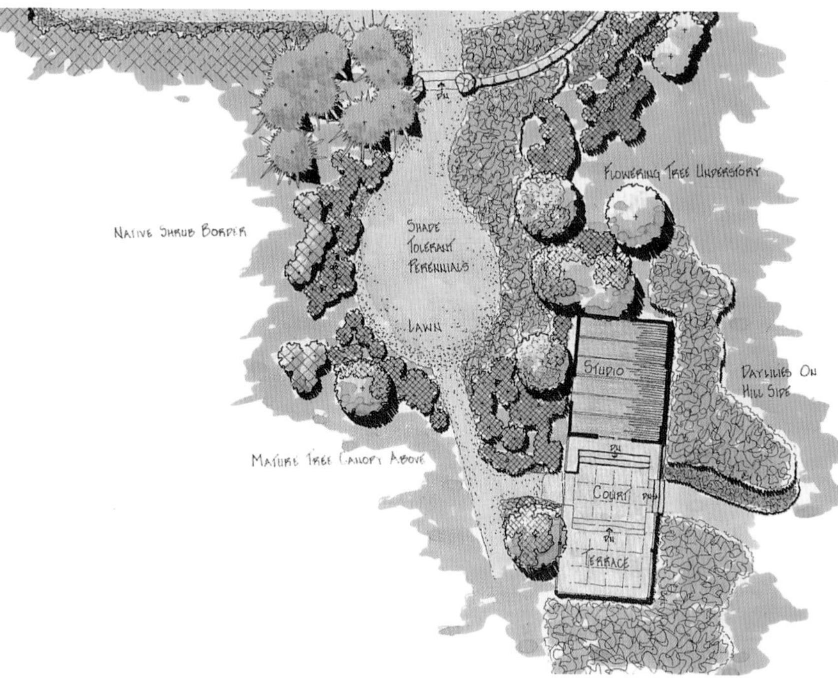

Right: Designed by the architectural firm of Truex Cullins and Partners, the writer's studio rests beneath a dense canopy of mature sugar maples and red oaks.

Bottom: A view through the terrace past the stone entry court to the studio.

POOL GARDEN

Samuel H. Williamson

In a leafy suburb of Dedham, Massachusetts, an 1850s Greek revival house sits atop a small hill in the woods. Beneath an immense copper beech tree in the backyard, an oval swimming pool is almost entirely surrounded by stone walls in a tight, 30-by-37-foot space.

To accentuate the pool and give coherency to the lawn panels that flank it, the landscape architect encircled the pool with bluestone banding that twists and threads its way through the terrace. The spaces between bands become lawn panels, stone infill, or planting pockets. The stone infill between bands is a veined slate with blue colors similar to the colors of the bluestone. Ruddy purple veins in the slate recalling the color of the copper beech.

BIG IDEA:

Plantings echoing the colors of the beech were chosen by the landscape architect. Reddish colored flowers are often neglected because they appear "brown" to some people; here they go exceptionally well with the color of the beech. The stems and undersides of the leaves of *Ligularia dentata*, the flowers of *Fritillaria meleagris*, the leaves of red-leafed rose *Rosa rubrifolia* and purple smokebush *Cotinus coggygria* "Royal purple" are set off by the white Casablanca lilies, white tulips, daffodils, and an espaliered magnolia along the stone wall.

Right: By surrounding the pool and lawn panels with the same bluestone used for the terrace, the small backyard becomes a coherent whole.

Photography: Adrian Catalano

Left: The border passes from full sun, with tulips in spring to full shade with *Astilboides tabularis.*

Right, top: Espaliered peaches help achieve a full range of heights in a tight border.

Right, bottom: An Ezra Pound peony embodies the deep red and white color scheme early in the spring.

GARDEN PLAN

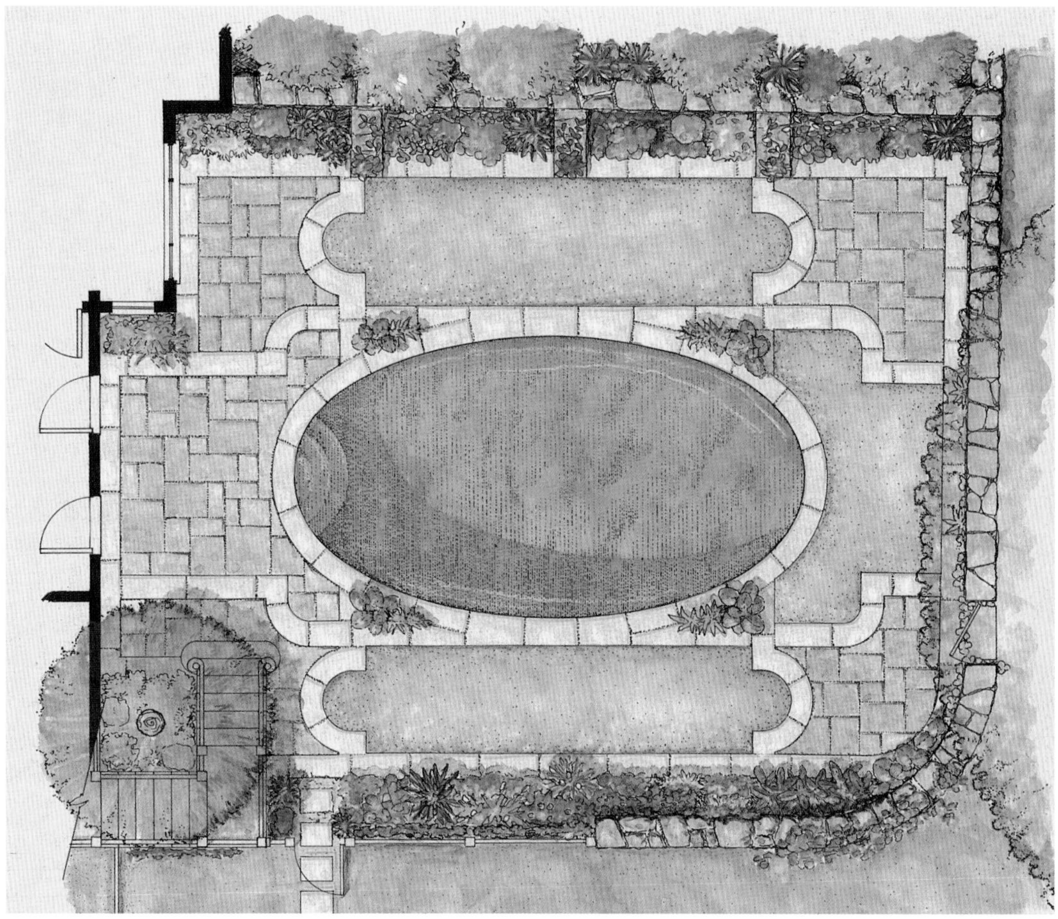

Left: The dark red leaves of the *Heuchera* "Purple Palace" echo the colors of the copper beech and Japanese maple in the distance.

Right: A bench at the edge of the garden.

SEASONAL GARDEN

Oehme, van Sweden& Associates

An important feature of this townhouse garden is its gentle slope up toward the back. The theatrical quality of its "raked stage" provides the basis for mystery and visual depth. The back of the house was opened up with French doors so that the kitchen flows into the garden. Located just outside the kitchen is a very narrow terrace, only 7 feet deep. The plantings seem to come right up to the house, virtually at eye level from the kitchen table. Layers of plants in the foreground meander toward the garden path and leads the eye deeper into a scene never completely revealed despite the restricted space. This modest garden changes character with the seasons.

BIG IDEA: Because of the dense plantings in a relatively small area, this garden functions best as a viewing garden, to be seen at eye level from the kitchen and above from the bedroom. With careful selection and placement of plants, hardscape, and sculpture, it is a constant visual feast changing with the seasons. Careful lighting allows it to maintain its appeal on the darkest of nights.

Left: As viewed from the kitchen, the dense garden foliage is at eye level. A small terrace allows for intimate dining and gives the sense of being inside the garden.

Above: A ceramic garden ornament.

Photography: James van Sweden

GARDEN PLAN

Previous pages: Over 800 spring bulbs are planted every year. The sculpture is by Grace Knowlton.

Below: A view from the garden to the kitchen.

Right: The garden's character remains strong even in the winter.

GARDEN ARCHITECTURE

Charles Warren

This tiny garden was created in a small walled area behind a Georgian style townhouse on the west side of Manhattan. It is organized into three connected "rooms", each characterized by different architectural elements. The garden is entered through the first room, a long gallery flanked with raised planting beds of hosta. Along the west wall of the gallery are salvaged, cast iron seals of the City of New York. The gallery terminates at an open pavilion defined by Corinthian columns supporting wrought iron arches. This structure forms a link between the gallery and the main garden room. This room is defined by a brick wall topped with a wooden trellis. Lilac and gray bluestone pavers create a pattern throughout the garden. The columns and the trellis are cedar. Because of its location, the garden is planted with shade-tolerant hosta and varieties of ivy.

BIG IDEA: The trellis serves a number of purposes. It screens from view the utility wires outside the garden while diminishing the subterranean aura. It also serves to frame the garden when viewed from the upper level apartment windows. The end wall of the trellis contains a mirrored arch, creating the illusion of a distant view.

Above: The mirrored arch in the trellis.

Right: Upon entering the garden, the first room is a long gallery with raised planting beds of hosta. A salvaged, cast iron seal of the City of New York is on the west wall.

Photography: Mick Hales

Left: The gallery terminates in an open pavilion of Corinthian columns surmounted by wrought iron arches.

Right: Architectural details used in the garden's design.

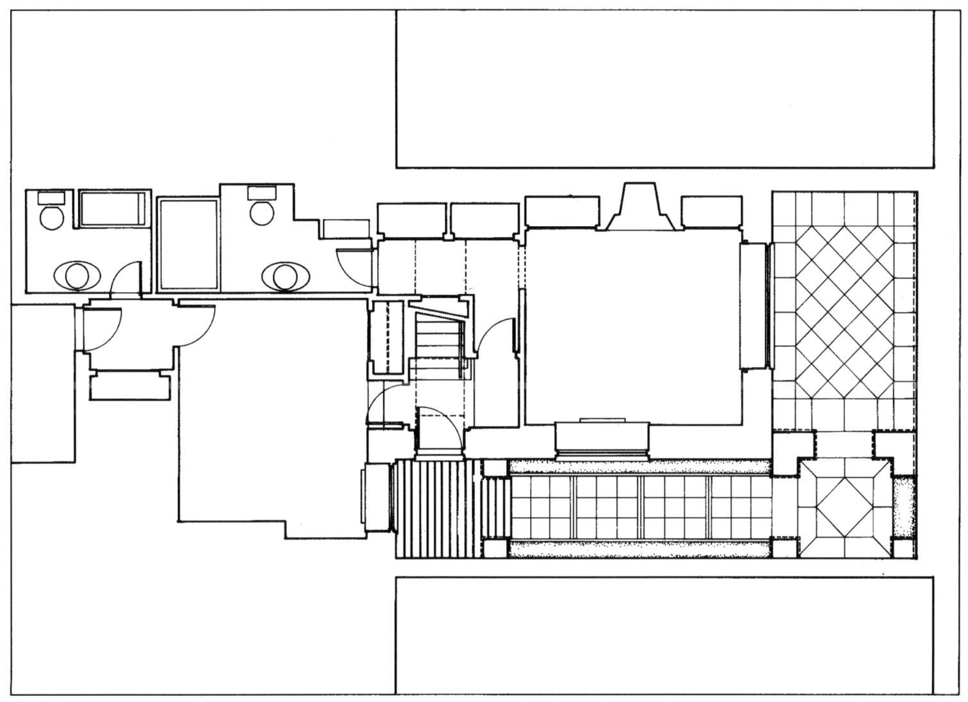

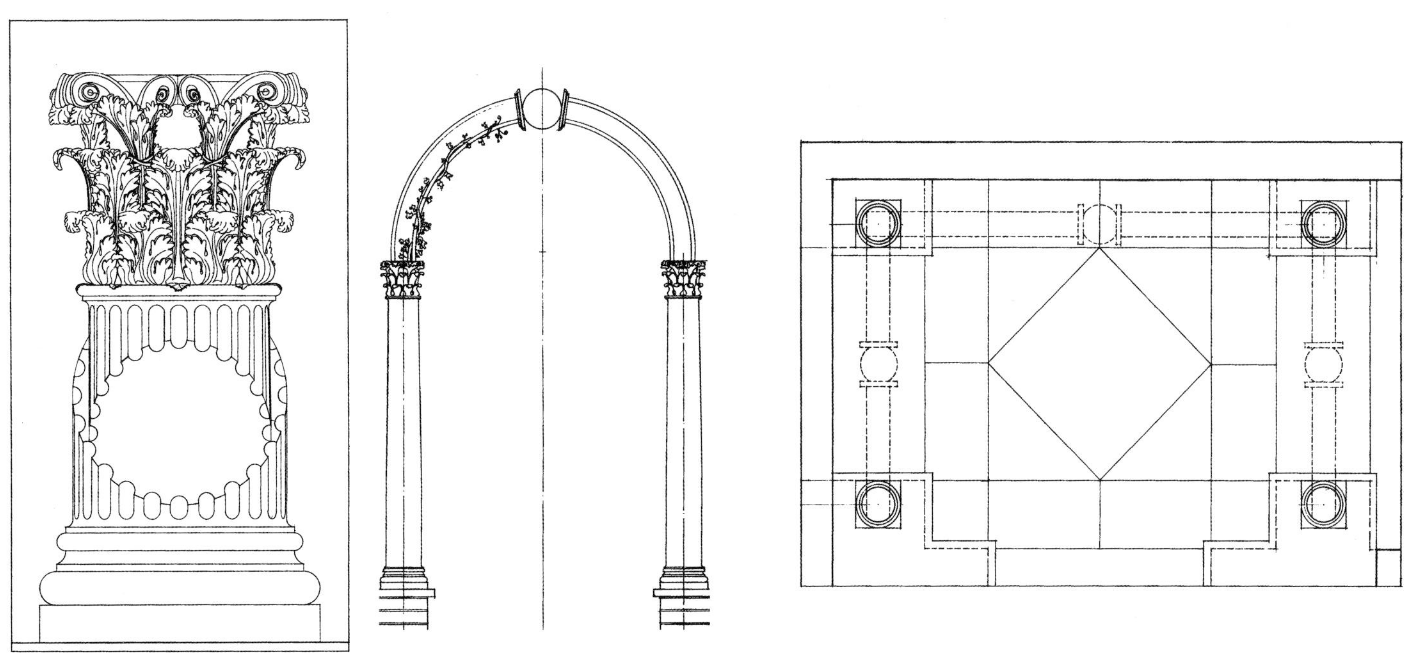

Left: A brick wall capped with a wooden trellis is a focal point in the main garden room. The mirrored arch creates the illusion of a distant view.

FRONT YARD FOR TWO

Floor & Associates, Inc.

Located in an historic neighborhood of 1920s and 1930s bungalows, this residence was one of the few on its block without a front porch. Rather than add one, the owners decided on a semi-private front yard patio that would reflect the simple architectural lines and materials of the house.

The patio designed by the landscape architects is only 10-feet square, and constructed on a raised pad of Mexican canterra stone. When viewed from the street, the patio seems to float above a bed of seasonal desert wildflowers. A low thick wall separates the patio from the front yard on two sides. The semi-deciduous Chilean mesquite tree provides thick shade during the summer and filtered light during the winter.

BIG IDEA: The front patio was designed to function as a semi-private seating area as well as the residence's main entry. Prior to remodeling, the entry was from the side, off the driveway and somewhat hidden by a large hedge of overgrown myrtle. The existing front landing was removed and replaced with an architectural bent which visually frames the entry and the driveway while extending the strong horizontal lines of the house itself. The patio was separated from the driveway by a wide entry path of hand carved Mexican canterra stone pavers and a low, at-grade planter.

Right: The patio floats in a sea of annual desert wildflowers.

Photography: Christopher Brown

Left: The patio affords a panoramic view of the neighborhood.

Right: The 10-foot square patio is built on a raised pad of hand-carved Mexican canterra stone pavers.

GARDEN PLAN

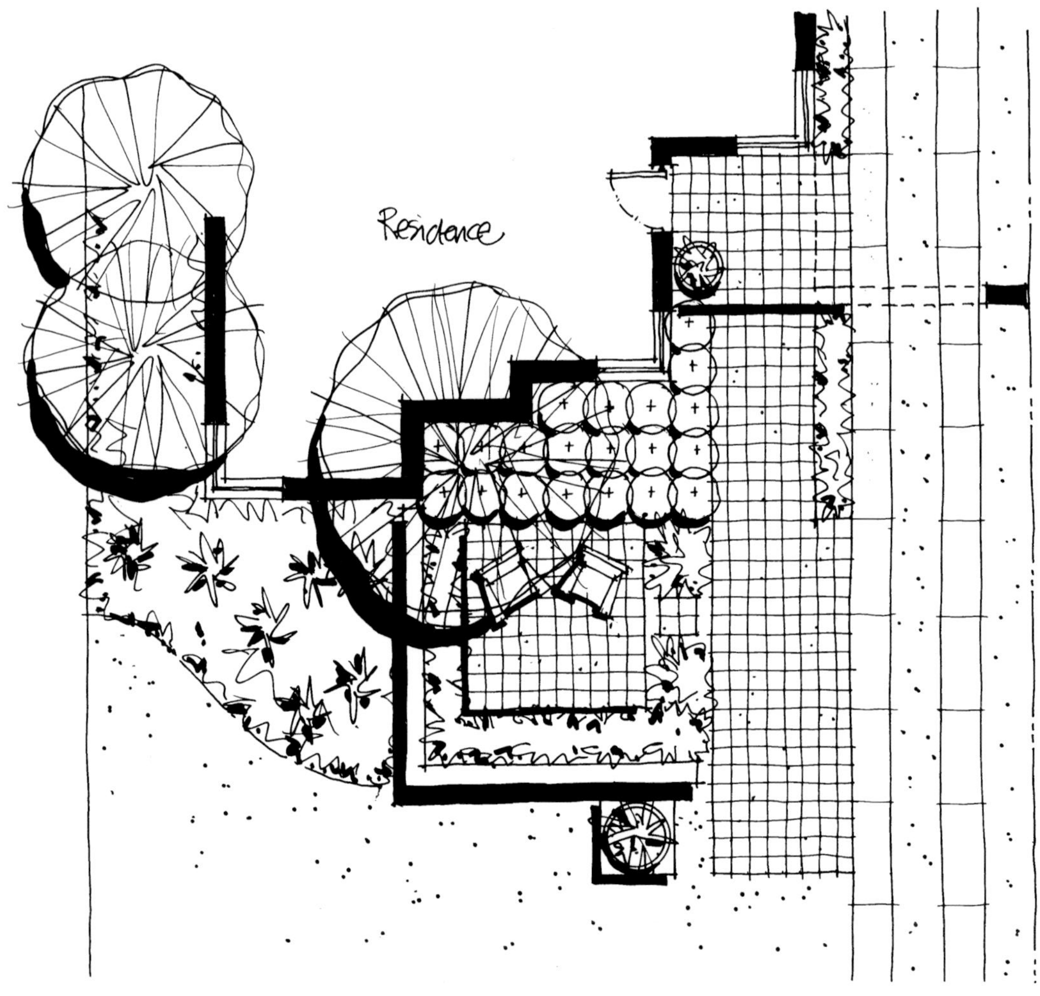

Right: A semi-deciduous Chilean mesquite tree offers thick shade during the summer and filtered light during the winter.

THE GLASS GARDEN

Andrew Cao

The Glass Garden is a garden of memories. When the Vietnamese-born landscape architect was ten years old, his family moved from busy, urban Saigon to his grandmother's farm. There, he found himself surrounded by ancient as well as contemporary icons: vast rice fields set in a patchwork grid of mud banks; salt farms with their surreal expanses of white cones reflecting in the changing light; and giant metal skeletons of rusting armaments left over from the war which today still dot the Vietnamese countryside. All of these images are incorporated in this garden.

BIG IDEA: Forty-five tons of recycled glass in five different colors helped the landscape architect realize this garden of memories. The plant palette is simple and includes lemon grass, stipa (representing rice), banana, agave, cannas, and orchids. White cones of glass recalling the salt farms, are lighted from below with fiber optic fixtures. The recycled glass enhances the sculptural quality of plant materials and brings vibrant new colors to the garden.

Right: The main pathway inside the front gate winds through "rice mounds" of crushed, recycled bottle glass. The glass-embedded wall extends the full depth of the property. Cobalt blue "ocean waves" represent the Vietnamese coast line.

Photography: Stephen Jerrom

Left: Eleven "salt cones", lit from below with fiber optic lighting, create a surreal yet peaceful reflecting pond. Glass-embedded concrete "mud banks" enclose the pond and four "rice" terraces.

Right: Mexican feather grass growing in a bed of cobalt blue glass depicts flooded rice paddies.

GARDEN PLAN

Top: A sculpture by Ann McKenna recalls the rusting war armaments in the Vietnamese countryside.

Right: Glass cones appear weightless in the reflecting pond.

INNER COURTYARDS

Ron Herman

This Japanese-influenced courtyard garden can be observed from several levels and from a variety of locations within the house. A small entry garden shields the property from the noise and distractions of the nearby street. Here, the landscape architect has fashioned a modern, abstract interpretation of the Japanese ceremonial water basin, *tsukubai*, often found in temple gardens. The main progression from the entry garden to the living space is via a glass gallery overlooking the courtyard garden. The checkerboard pattern of black riverwash stones, moss, and limestone pavers was inspired by a pattern the landscape architect first viewed at a Zen temple in Kyoto.

BIG IDEA: This contemporary interpretation of a Zen garden uses bronze edging to create a clean, rigid grid with raised steps above a small bamboo grove underplanted with mondo grass. Elevation changes increase the sense of space and enhance visual interest. Another important element in this garden is water. In Japanese landscapes, water is valued for its soothing sounds and reflective qualities. Here, a perfect reflective sheet of water spills over the edge of a rimless pool at the south end of the garden. When viewed directly from the living room this sheer sheet of water imparts sparkle and depth to the surrounding site.

Above: A detail of the cast glass screen with patterns reminiscent of artist Piet Mondrian's work.

Right: Access to the garden from behind a glass screen delays relevation of the site's full impact. The reflecting pool is adjacent to the screen.

Photography: Mark Schwartz

GARDEN PLAN

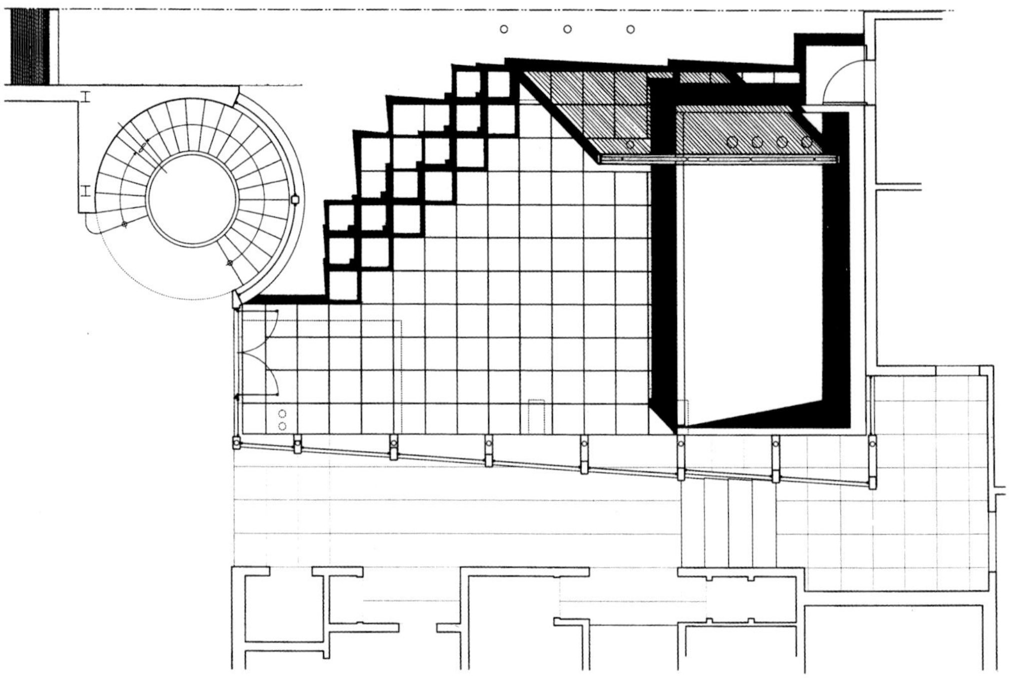

Previous pages: A view of the courtyard from the second floor.

Left: Detail of moss and riverwash stones contained within the bronze edging of the courtyard.

Right: The change in elevation within the courtyard enhances the sense of space.

Left: In the entry garden, water flows down a cable over the rock and into a water basin.

Right: The rock, which serves as the water basin, is suspended in midair.

Photographs: Ron Herman

CARPET OF MOSS

Sheela Lampietti & Joseph Krakora

BIG IDEA:

Water, or the concept of water, is essential in a Japanese garden. Its tranquil sounds and reflective qualities are highly regarded. A water wall adjacent to the terrace was designed for this garden in a collaborative effort among the landscape designer, the owner, and a ceramic artist.

Measuring 10 feet high by 5 feet wide, the entire wall is comprised of black- and rust-colored tiles; fired in an ancient Japanese wood-fired method, the result is a random color variation. The wall is angled out at the base to delay the flow of water that cascades from the top. The shimmering water adds depth to the side of the terrace while providing a soothing sound in this garden of contemplation.

The aesthetics of Japanese garden design had a powerful influence on this project. Using a spare and carefully controlled palette of plants, stones, water, and ornaments, this small urban garden becomes a place of contemplation and mystery. While appearing quite ancient, the garden is only a few years old. A path that bisects the space is swept frequently, exposing and accentuating the roots of trees. The deep black soil contrasts sharply with rich green moss. The path meanders like a fresh-water stream from the terrace to a wooden shed where the eye is drawn to a Noguchi paper lantern glowing softly through the shed's window.

The owner's collection of antique Japanese rice stones and American millstones are carefully arranged to enhance spatial depth in the garden. The largest millstone is prominently placed under the shed's window at the end of the path.

Left: A box turtle named "Sarge", calls this garden his home.
Photograph: Joseph Krakora

Right: The garden viewed from the dining room terrace. The carpet of moss is accentuated by a variety of ferns. Hart's tongue fern, lady fern, and painted fern are seen here.

Photography: Roger Foley

GARDEN PLAN

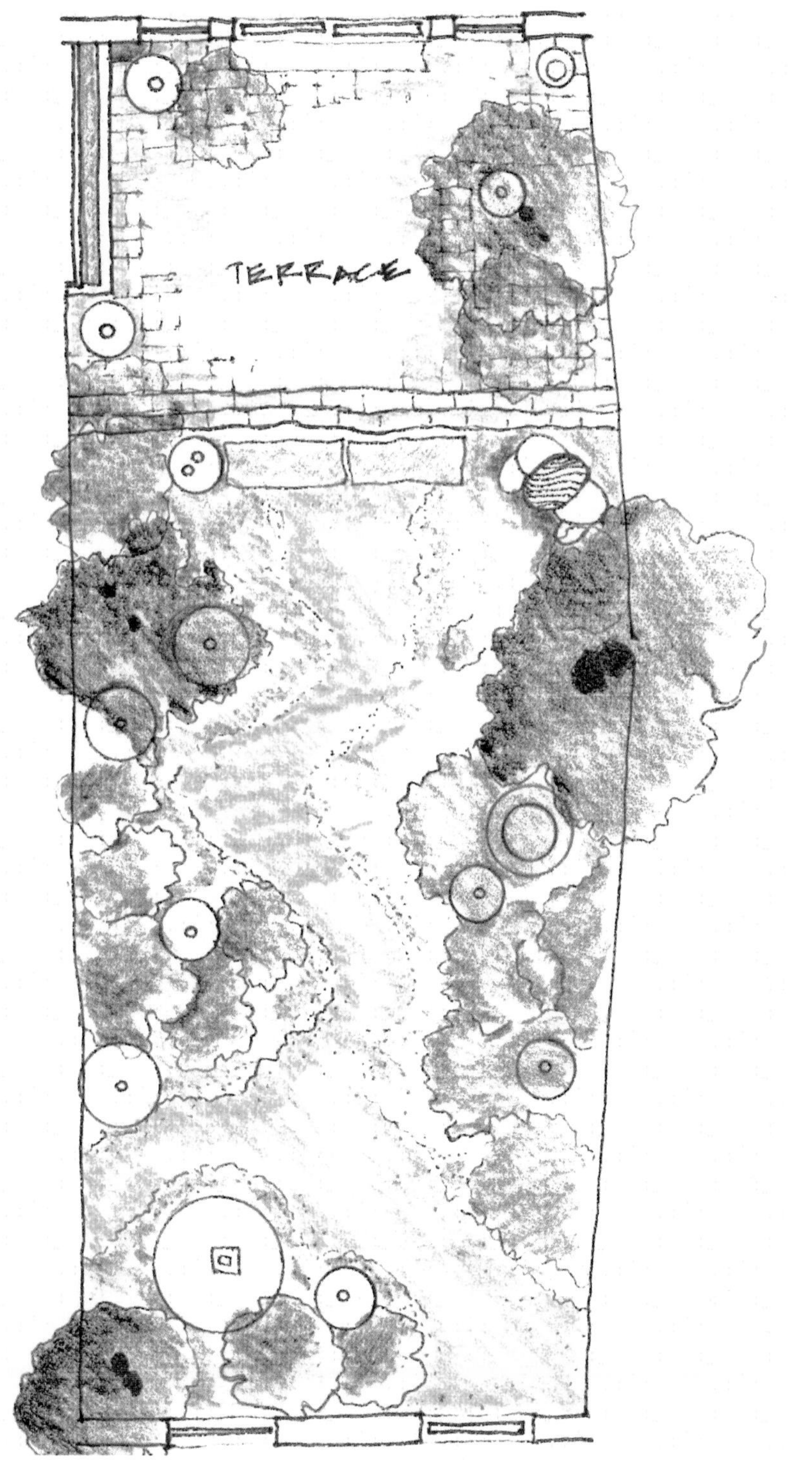

Right: A stone water basin is surrounded by wood ferns and azaleas.

Left: The water wall tiles were created by ceramic artist, Fred Hetzel.

Right: The Noguchi lamp is constantly on, drawing one's eye to the back of the garden. The Japanese maple frames the view.

ALUMINUM GARDEN

Ken Smith

BIG IDEA: This simple urban garden rejects metaphor and narrative content in favor of using contemporary materials and plantings as media. The direct and beautiful expression of materials creates a garden of perceptual qualities: lightness and darkness, reflectivity, transparency, depth, movement, and growth.

This L-shaped, 585-square-foot rear courtyard is structured around an existing mature maple tree. The garden area steps back in a series of shallow terraces held by heavy timbers that are stained aluminum. The timber structure supports panels of industrial grating that are placed over common "trap rock" (crushed stone fill). As viewed from the townhouse, the garden has a forced perspective emphasized by the "tilting" effect of stepped terraces and the skewed garden edge. Running along this edge, a water runnel made of marine aluminum channel, steps down the terraces. A bamboo grove defines two sides of the garden and an expanded aluminum screen defines the third side. Commercial aluminum kitchen supply pots serve as planters for flowering vines.

A 115-square-foot terrace on the third floor overlooks the garden. A painted aluminum floor, a planter with grasses, and an expanded aluminum screen structure the space and frame views from this elevated position. Two illuminated acrylic columns provide an ambient glow for the garden spaces.

Right: The garden terraces create usable areas for sitting, dining, and socializing. The industrial timbers create the terraces which are in-filled with industrial panels of fiberglass grating that are placed over crushed stone.

Photography: Betsy Pinover Schiff

GARDEN PLAN

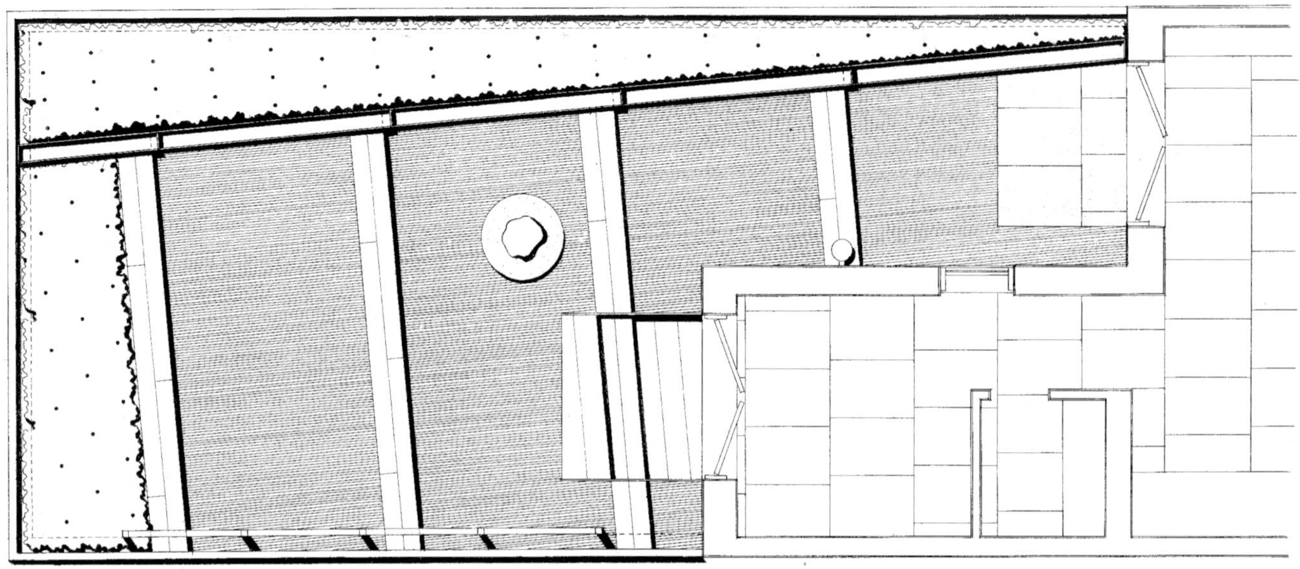

UPPER TERRACE

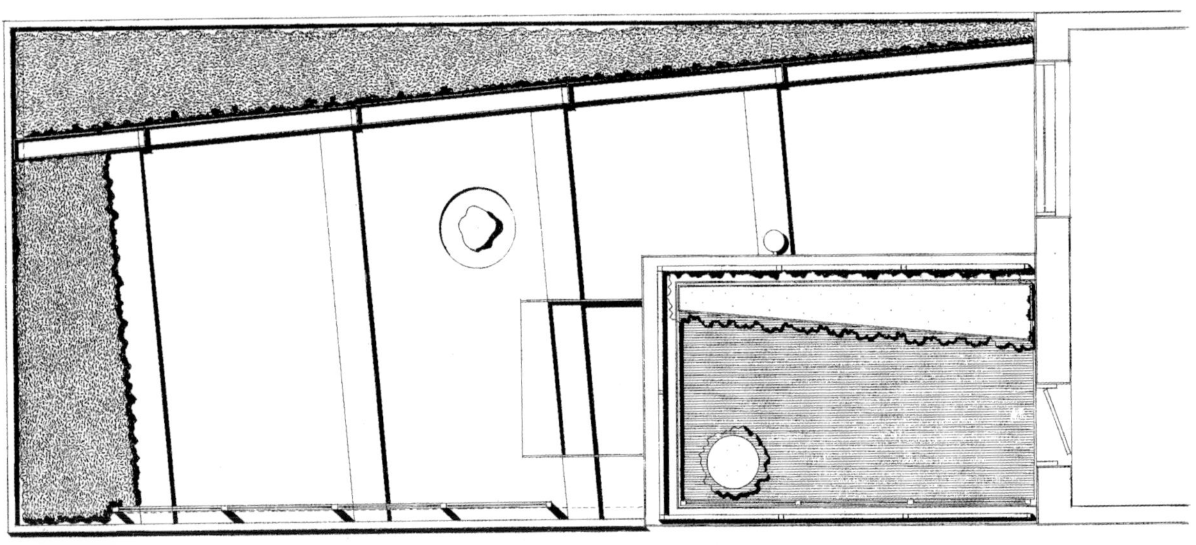

STACKED ELEVATION

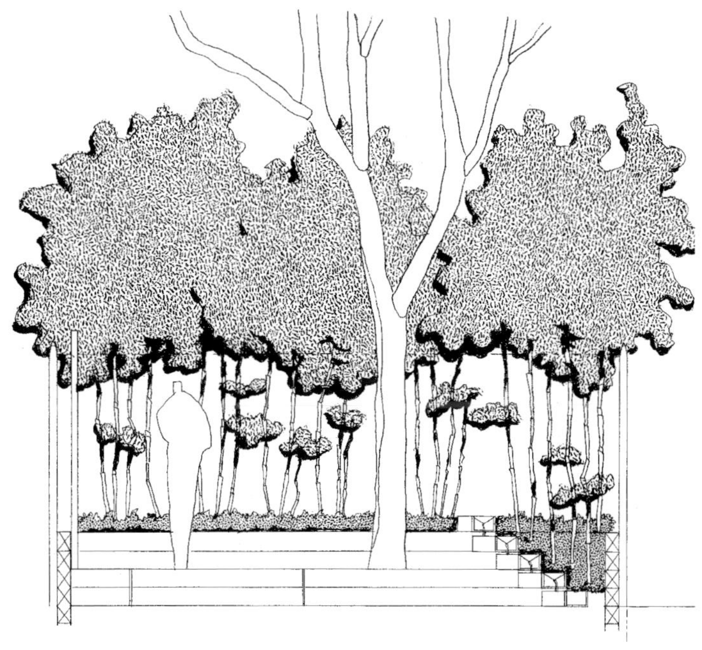

SECTION

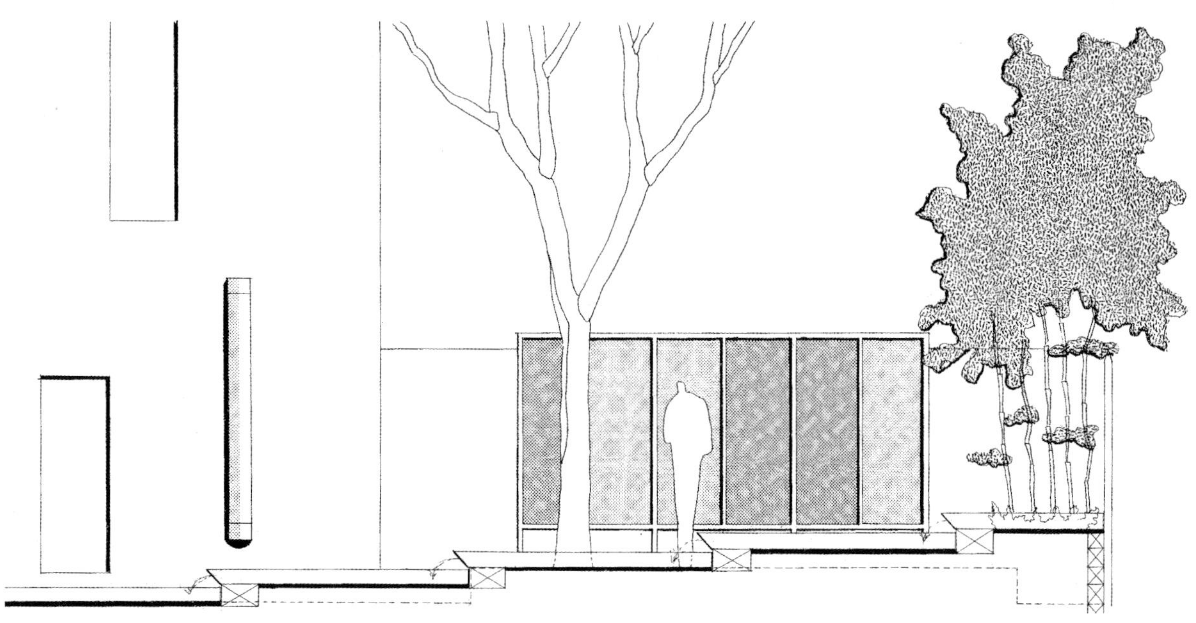

Left: The effect of the forced perspective created by the stepped terraces and skewed edge is apparent in this view from the dining room and kitchen. This slight-of-hand illusion extends to living space of the house into the garden, creating the perception that the garden is larger than it actually is.

Right: The commercial aluminum cooking pots are planted with clematis, which will be trained to grow up the aluminum screen to create a vertical wall of seasonal flowers.

Left (top): The water runnel that steps down the garden terraces provides a visual sparkle, an audible splash, and animation for the garden.

Left (bottom): The waterspout is the source for the fountain runnel. The landscape architect was inspired by sink faucets in restaurants.

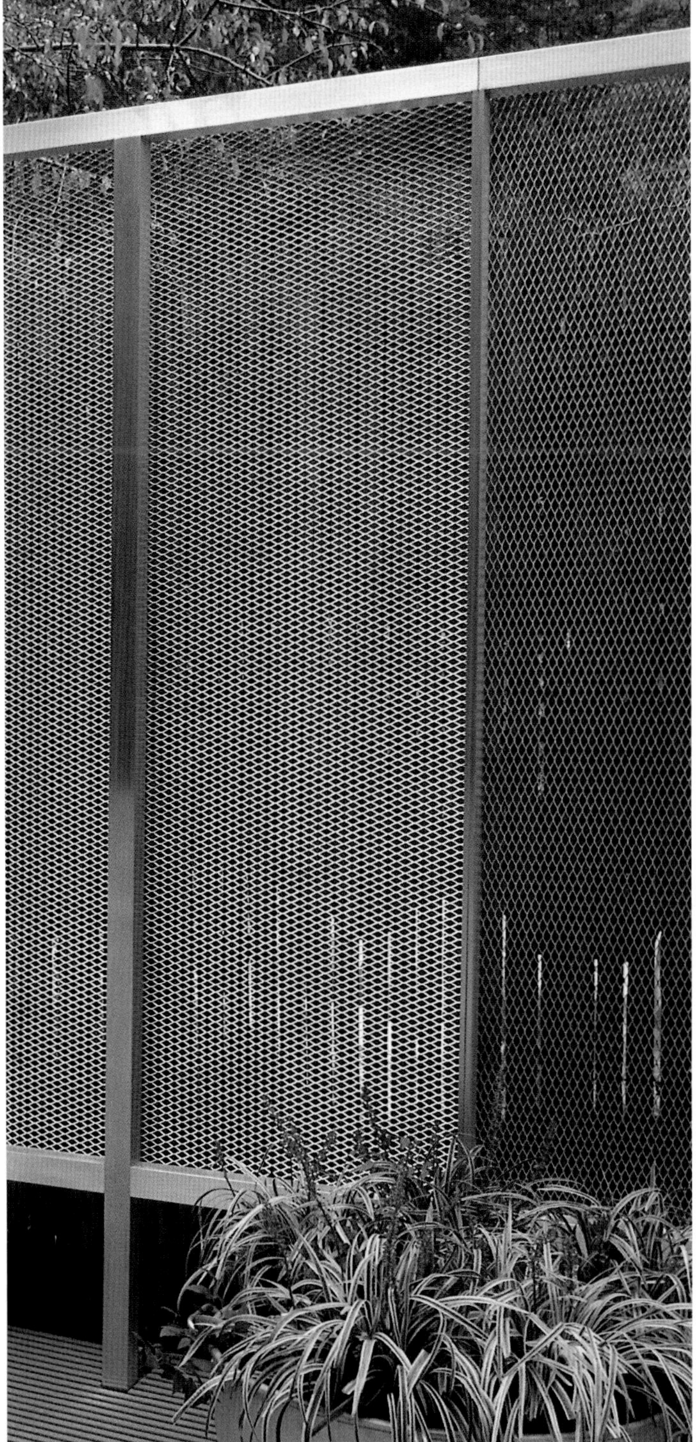

Right: The glowing column produces an ambient glow in the garden.

Far right: The aluminum screen is fabricated using two directions of expanded aluminum material to create variable textures and shadow patterns.

BORROWED VIEW

Mia Lehrer & Associates

This project involved the remodeling of a Bel-Air, California house and garden with dramatic city and canyon views. The client wanted the architect and landscape architect to strengthen the relationship between the house, the garden, and the views.

An entry court and path with rich plantings replaced the driveway and concrete paving. Through a symbolic opening in a curving wall, a stone path from the garage leads to the house's entrance. A gravel strip with rain chains suspended from the roof provides an intense textural contrast with the smooth plaster walls along the house's exterior edge.

BIG IDEA:

The plantings are colorful, sculptural, and texturally varied. Existing olive trees, agaves, and eucalyptus were preserved. New plant materials were selected to frame and punctuate the extraordinary views, as well as to create borders and shade. The blue/gray foliage agaves and Westringia complement the house's warm colors.

Above and Right: The city and the canyon provide dramatic backdrops for this property. Plants are chosen to frame and punctuate the vista.

Photography: Steve Gunther

Left: The stone path from the garage leads to a symbolic opening in the curving stucco wall. The warm colors of the house are complemented by the blue/gray sculptural plants.

Right: Plants and hardscape provide a variety of textures in the garden.

GARDEN PLAN

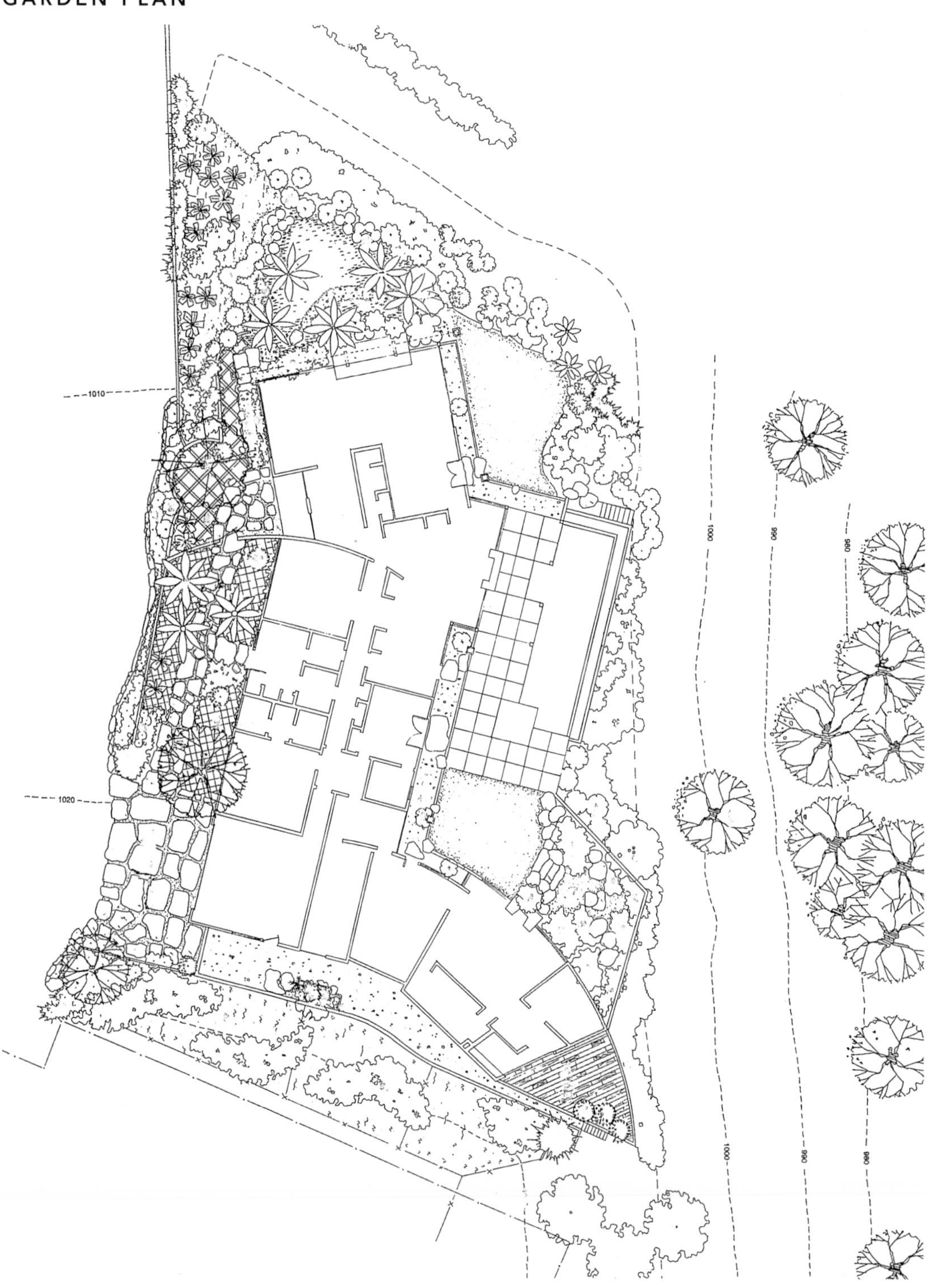

Right: *Chondropetulum tectorum* (cape rush) grows against the house.

Below: *Festuca ovina* (blue fescue) is planted outside the living room.

Left: Entrance to the house viewed from the hillside.

Right: Smooth stucco walls provide a neutral background for rough stones and *Cotoneaster lacteus*.

HILLTOP COTTAGE

Philip Metcalf & Patricia Galagan

Above: A decorative garden ornament surrounded by rhododendrons.

Right: View of the house from the lower terrace.

Photography: Philip Metcalf

BIG IDEA:

Water features dominate this garden. Two fish ponds–a formal one for Koi and an informal one for goldfish and rampant aquatic plants–anchor the site. Tsukubai, birdbaths, and stone basins reinforce the reflective and cooling theme of water. Keeping the pond water clean and suitable for fish and plants is achieved with state-of-the-art biological filtration systems. Water from the 2,500 gallon koi pond flows by gravity to three vortex filters that gently separate waste for easy removal; a tank with millions of plastic beads provides additional cleansing action. An ultraviolet light kills floating algae as the water is pumped back to the pond. Water in the 1,600 gallon goldfish pond, is pumped to a two-stage filter before it returns to the pond by gravity. Microbes, added to breakdown and neutralize waste in both ponds, ensure the health of fish and plants.

When the owners purchased this property, the garden and house were in poor condition having been neglected for many years. The derelict garden contained a variety of trees and shrubs that the owners rescued, and in many cases, transplanted. Building on existing stock, the garden was restored over a several year period into a series of linked rooms, creating an unusually rich and varied experience for such a compact space. The hilltop location required extensive terracing to accommodate the steep grade behind the house. An ornamental pool on the lower terrace was restored and converted to a fish pond; it is flanked by metal columns salvaged from the breezeway of the old house that was partially demolished and rebuilt according to a design by architect, Charles Moore. A second fish pond was built adjacent to the upper terrace. Stone was used throughout the garden for coping, terraces, paths, and drylaid walls.

Left: A sculptural stone divides the gravel path that leads to the kitchen terrace or lower garden.

Bottom: The goldfish pond's amorphous form softens the hard-edged bluestone terrace. Water lilies, iris, thalia, and parrot's feather shelter fish and frogs.

Right: A bamboo water pipe and a natural stone basin at the edge of the goldfish pond are surrounded by polished gray river stones.

GARDEN PLAN

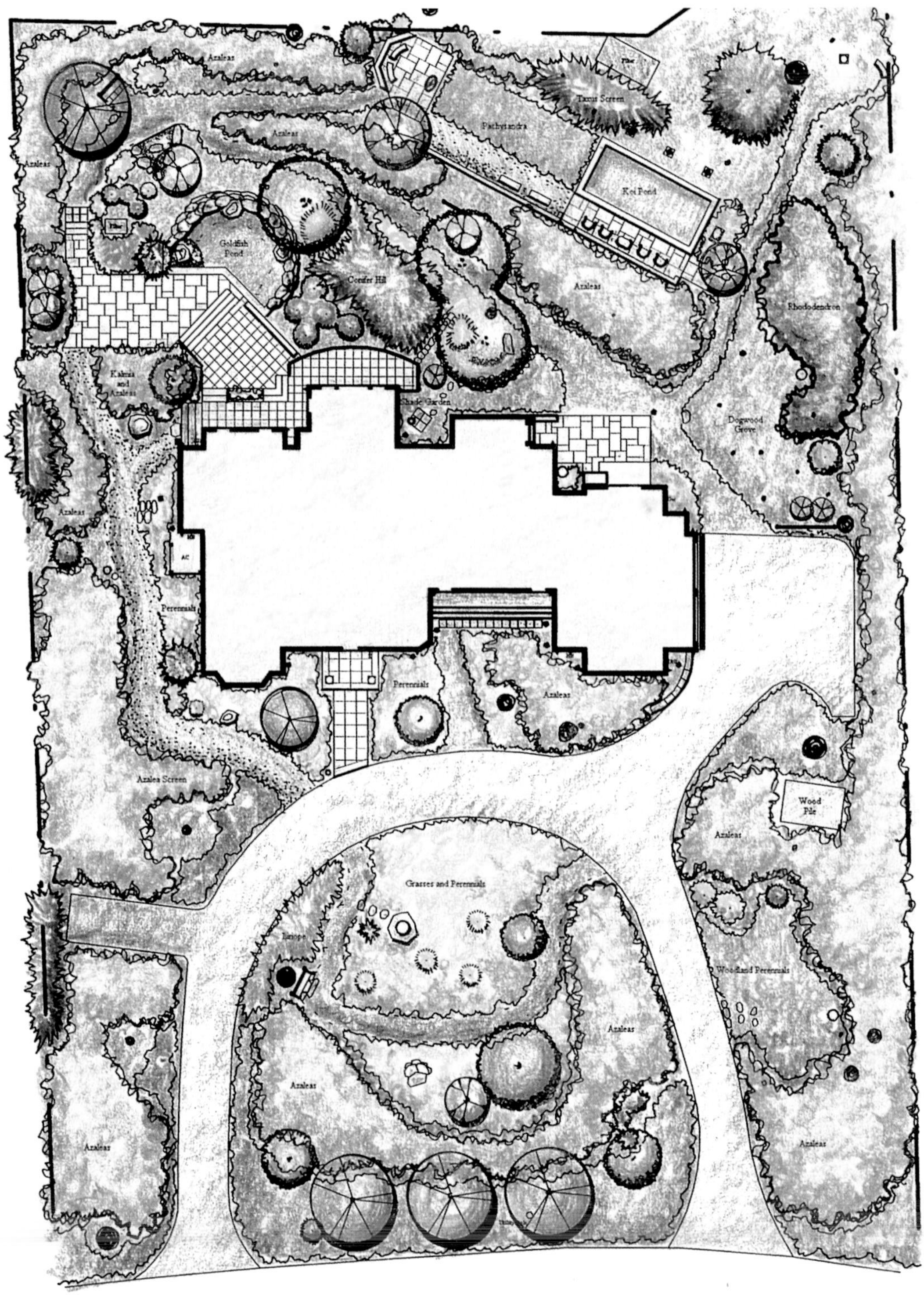

Azaleas
Azaleas
Azaleas
Pachysandra
Taxus Screen
Koi Pond
Filter
Goldfish Pond
Conifer Hill
Azaleas
Rhododendron
Kalmia and Azaleas
Shade Garden
Dogwood Grove
Azaleas
AC
Perennials
Perennials
Azaleas
Azalea Screen
Wood Pile
Azaleas
Grasses and Perennials
Woodland Perennials
Azaleas
Azaleas
Azaleas
Azaleas

Right: Secluded seating area features antique curved benches that were found on the property.

Bottom: Replacing the front lawn, a perennial garden shelters the house from the street. The tall birdbath is made from an antique chimney flue topped by a broad copper basin.

Left: The koi pond is surrounded by metal columns taken from a section of the old house when it was rebuilt.

TROPICAL RETREAT

Raymond Jungles

The design of this garden is a collaboration between the landscape architect and his wife, an artist known for her outdoor murals. The garden was created in conjunction with the renovation of the house.

Usable exterior space has been maximized leaving compact areas for planting. Shade is provided by several red Spicata coconut palms, hurricane palms, cabbage palms, and numerous other tropical species. A louvered privacy fence was constructed around the property to shield it from the dense Key West, Florida neighborhood where it is located. Color was judiciously applied to the paving surfaces and vertical planes of the walls, enlivening the spaces and adding depth to the garden. A stately, mature Mahogany tree anchors the garden.

BIG IDEA: The swimming pool was built adjacent to the newly renovated living area and kitchen and is a prominent feature in the garden visible from many areas of the house. It is designed not only for a refreshing dip, but also as a major design element. It is flanked by a colorful mural by Debra Yates which also contains a fountain that brings the soothing sound of falling water into the garden, masking nearby street noises. The pool is surfaced with a gray Diamond Brite to give it the look of a lagoon, making it highly reflective during the day, bringing the sky into the garden.

Above: A detail of the mural by Debra Yates.

Right: The swimming pool serves multiple purposes in this small tropical garden.

Photography: Raymond Jungles

Left: A view of the pool from the entrance to the house designed by Jungles and Yates. Sight lines were maintained so that the entire length of the property is visible from the entry. The poured-in-place, rock salt-textured, patina-finished concrete panels float in a "pool" of Mexican river rocks.

Right: A detail of the fountain, looking across the swimming pool toward the exterior living space.
Photograph: Lanny Provo

Right: A louvered privacy fence surrounds the entire property. Perimeter planting outside the fence is primarily indigenous leafy shrubs and small trees, chosen for their fragrant qualities. Photograph: Lanny Provo

GARDEN PLAN

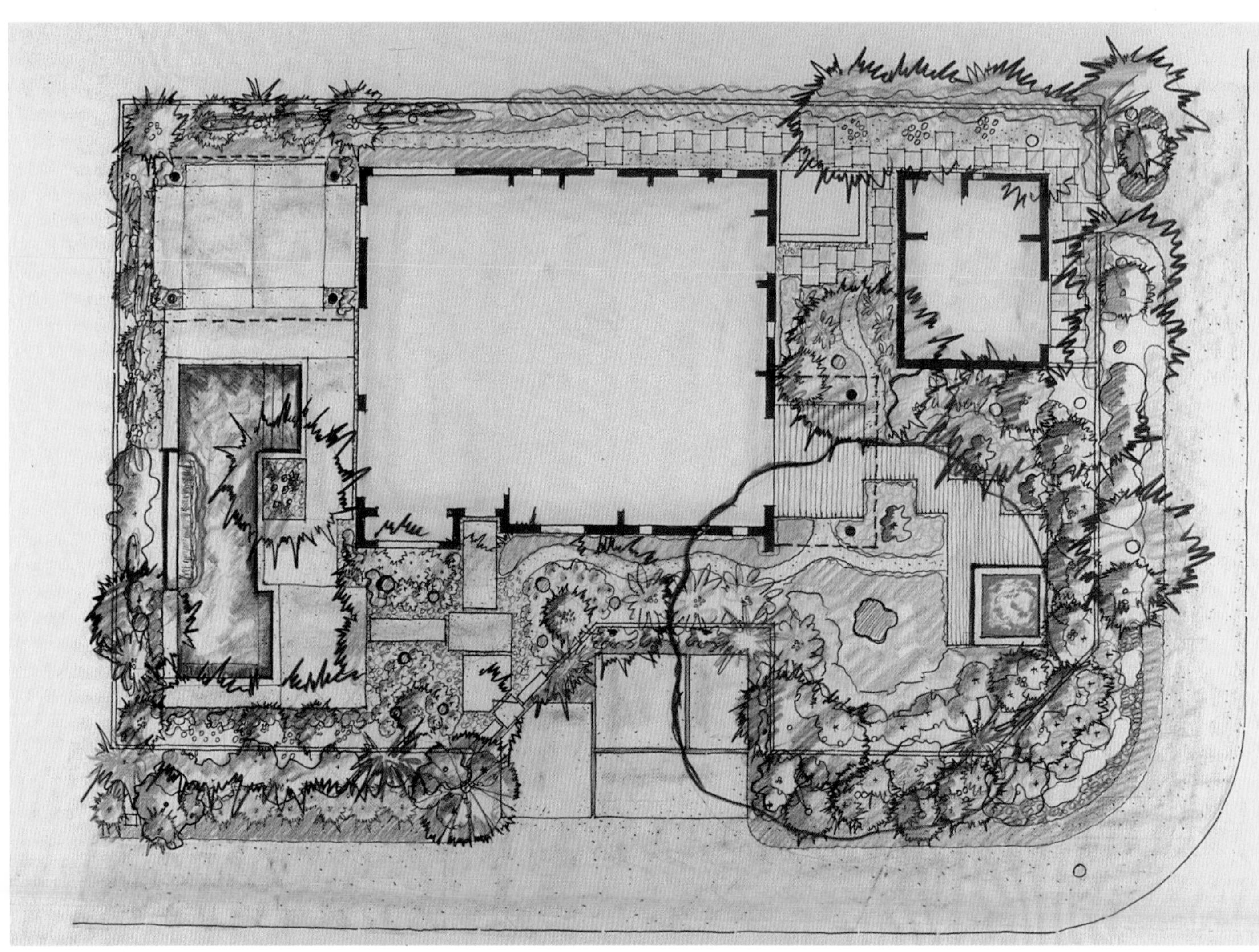

Above: A view of the covered exterior living space.

Left: An outdoor shower extends the master bath into the garden. It is shaded by a large *Phoenix sylvestris*, (Wild Silver Date Palm).
Photograph: Lanny Provo

SUSTAINABLE GARDEN

Mario Schjetnan

This garden is located in Malinalco, Mexico, an exuberant subtropical valley 100 miles southwest of Mexico City. The house and garden were designed by the landscape architect within the context of of this historic Mexican town's semirural setting. The subtropical climate and the goal to establish a strong relationship with the surrounding landscape directed the layout of the living room, dining room, and kitchen space as a covered open terrace with a fireplace for cool nights. The L-shaped house plan creates a central courtyard in the Mexican tradition. In this courtyard, many elements of nature are present: water, soil, plants, sky, as well as birds, raccoons, and a few squirrels. The north-south axis is formed by a rill connecting a square fountain with a stone-carved still water mirror, reminiscent of Spanish and Moroccan gardens.

BIG IDEA: The garden is designed to recycle gray waters from the house back into the orchard through a sand filter. The pavement in the central patio is set on mud to filter rainwater. The pool holds rain water; when filled, it passes to the orchard and finally to an absorption well set on the third and lowest garden platform.

Right: The orchard garden is planted with coffee, avocado, tropical plum, banana, and lime trees.

Photography: Gabriel Figueroa

Left: The main patio is planted with guava trees. Rocks serve as the patio's paving material.

Right: The exterior corridor opens onto the courtyard. Entrances to the bedrooms are on the right.

GARDEN PLAN

Right: Lush plantings shade an outdoor dining area.

Below: A rill connects the rain collecting pool to the stone-carved still water mirror.

Left: Although small, the orchard has the appearance of a dense tropical jungle.

Above: The living room as seen from the central patio.

DIAGONAL LINES

Oehme, van Sweden & Associates

Space limitations in the backyard of a contemporary attached house dictated the garden design. The lap pool was placed to one side and screened from view from the house by a grove of river birch. The screening also allows for more privacy. Plantings were kept low at the rear of the property to take advantage of the extended view into the public park. The house sits on a high hill and in the winter months, the view extends to the river.

In addition to river birch, other major plant materials in the garden include perennials and ornamental grasses. There is a large *Zelkova serrata* for shade.

Boulders unearthed during construction were used to create a waterfall at the edge of the lily pool.

Above: Water ripples over stones unearthed during the construction of the house.

Right: An overview of the terrace and lily pond. Seat-height walls of the lily pond are capped with bluestone. Note the diagonal placement of the terrace relative to the wooden privacy fence.

Photography: James van Sweden

BIG IDEA:

The terrace and lily pool were designed as one piece, on the diagonal, in order to make this small garden appear much larger. In addition, the boards in the fence surrounding the property are placed on the diagonal to enlarge the apparent size of the garden.

Left: View of the terrace from the lily pool.

Right: View of the swimming pool. The diagonal placement of bluestone paving continues the motif established by the terrace and fence.

GARDEN PLAN

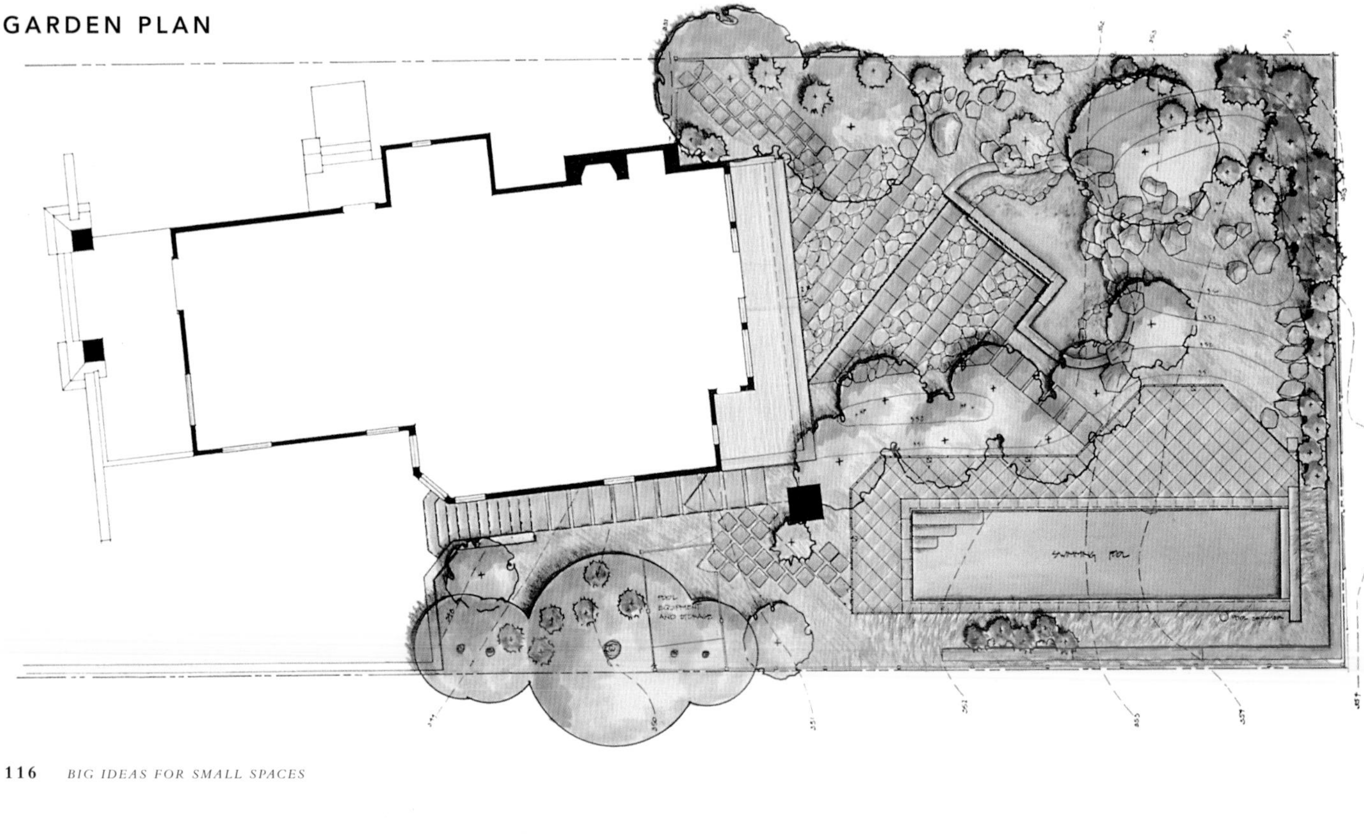

Left and right: Views of the terrace. A built-in lighting system under the seat wall's coping lights the terrace at the edge of the pool.

GARDEN PATHS

Michael Van Valkenburgh Associates, Inc.

On a site occupied by a traditional house, the owner/architect constructed a decidedly contemporary house on the lot behind it. He rented out the original dwelling and he and his wife, a concert pianist and teacher, moved into the contemporary dwelling. With two houses occupying the lot, the resulting garden space is long and narrow; an 8-foot grade exists between the back door and main entrance on the side of the contemporary house. The need for outdoor movement between these two entrances along with the strong orthogonal quality of the architecture greatly influenced the landscape architect's design for the garden. The landscape is treated "the way a constellation of stars forms around a space ship in the sky." Randomly placed bluestone pavers are arranged in front of each entrance. They are connected by a curving bluestone ramp that provides a gradual grade transition along the side of the house.

BIG IDEA: Oversized panels of fine-meshed chain link fencing run along the perimeter of the garden and parking area. This "animated wall" moves and flutters when the wind blows the suspended panels. Parts of the fence serve as a scrim for flowering vines during the summer months.

Right: A view of the ramp as it arcs up the slope from the rear of the house to the main entrance.

Photography: Charles Mayer

Left: Randomly placed bluestone pavers form a patio at the front side of the house.

Right: A view from the rear entrance looking up the ramp to the front of the garden.

GARDEN PLAN

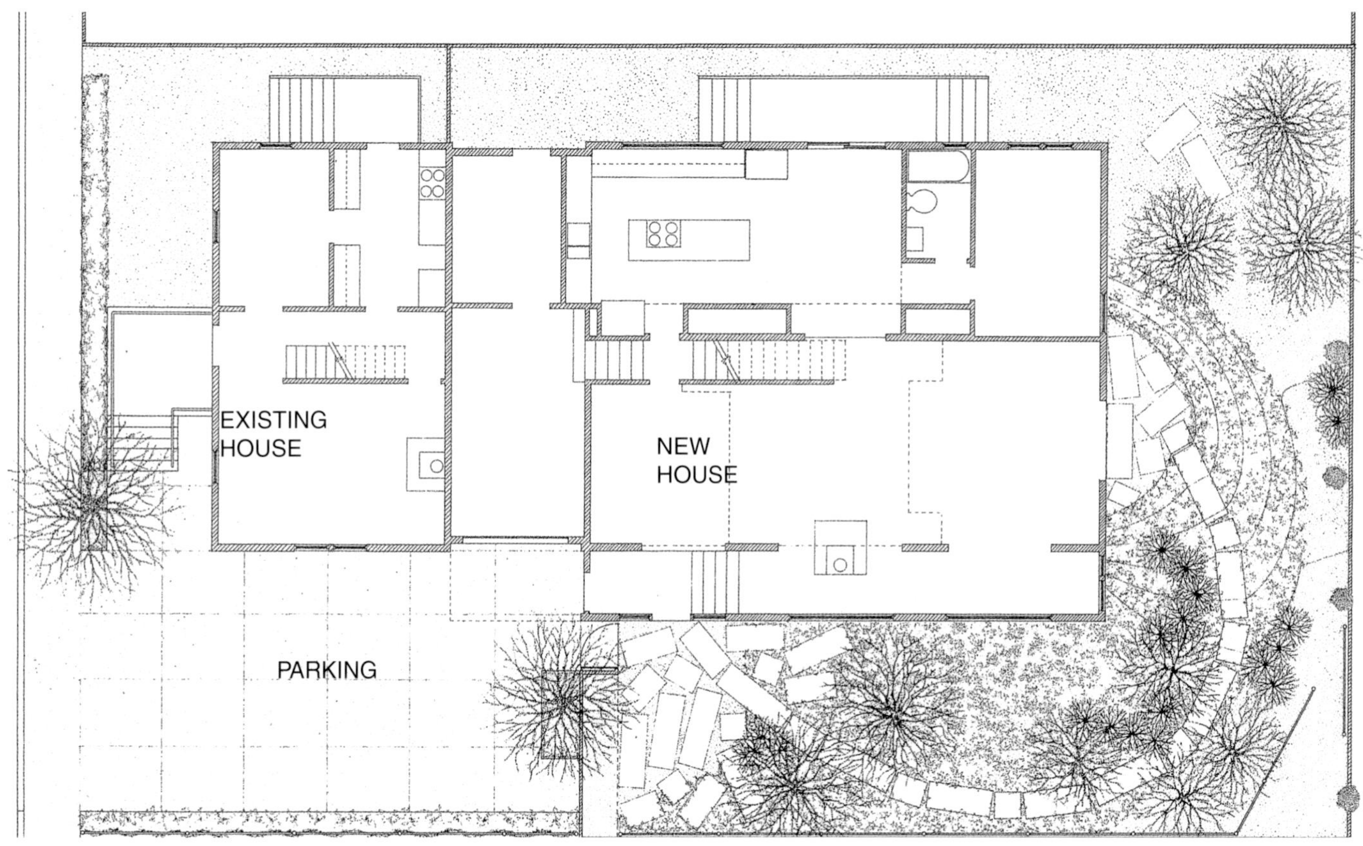

Right: The side entrance to the house features a "floating field" of bluestone pavers.

Far right: Oversized panels of a fine-meshed chain link create an "animated wall" around the garden and parking court area.

GARDEN SPACES

Mia Lehrer & Associates

Located in the Hollywood Hills, this is the home of a writer and artist. Rather than create one unified garden, the landscape architect devised a series of garden spaces and elements. These spaces draw the interiors outward and each functions according to its relationship with the house. A weeping fountain made of recycled concrete stands outside the master bedroom. The fountain recirculates water, audibly animating the small terrace. Other garden spaces include a rose garden and a vegetable garden. The hillside below is naturalized with white irises, perennial bulbs, and grasses. The owner finds inspiration in a writer's tower that overlooks these garden spaces.

BIG IDEA:

Of all the outdoor spaces in this garden, the most compelling is the outdoor shower. It allows for a genuine alfresco bathing experience because it is removed from the house and stands alone on the lawn. Framed by vine covered wire mesh walls, it looks like a piece of organic sculpture. A stone path leads from the house to the shower.

Above: A raised planting bed outside the master bedroom.
Photograph: Mia Lehrer

Right: The vine covered outdoor shower.
Photograph: Dominique Vorillon

Left and Right: A view of the master bedroom terrace. The weeping fountain is constructed of recycled concrete. Behind the wall the hillside is planted with irises, perennial bulbs, and grasses.

Photograph (left): Mia Lehrer

Photograph (right): Dominique Vorillon

GARDEN PLAN

GARDEN SHOWERS

Floor & Associates, Inc.

All of the patios and courtyards of this home are connected by brick walks and steps to provide easy circulation throughout the property. This private courtyard area is designed as an extension of the master bath. It contains an outdoor shower, and is screened from the rest of the property by a dark purple stucco wall covered with bougainvillea.

BIG IDEA:
This intimate space is lushly planted with moisture-tolerant plants including peppermint and spearmint which grow up between the pavers. They release wonderful refreshing fragrances when brushed against while showering. Aromatherapy at its best!

Right: The shower head is surrounded by bougainvillea and agaves.

Far Right: Lush plantings create a fragrant and private oasis for a refreshing outdoor shower.

Photography: Christopher Brown

Top: Single pane French doors lead from the master bath to the outdoor shower.

Left: Spearmint and peppermint are planted between the pavers of the shower floor.

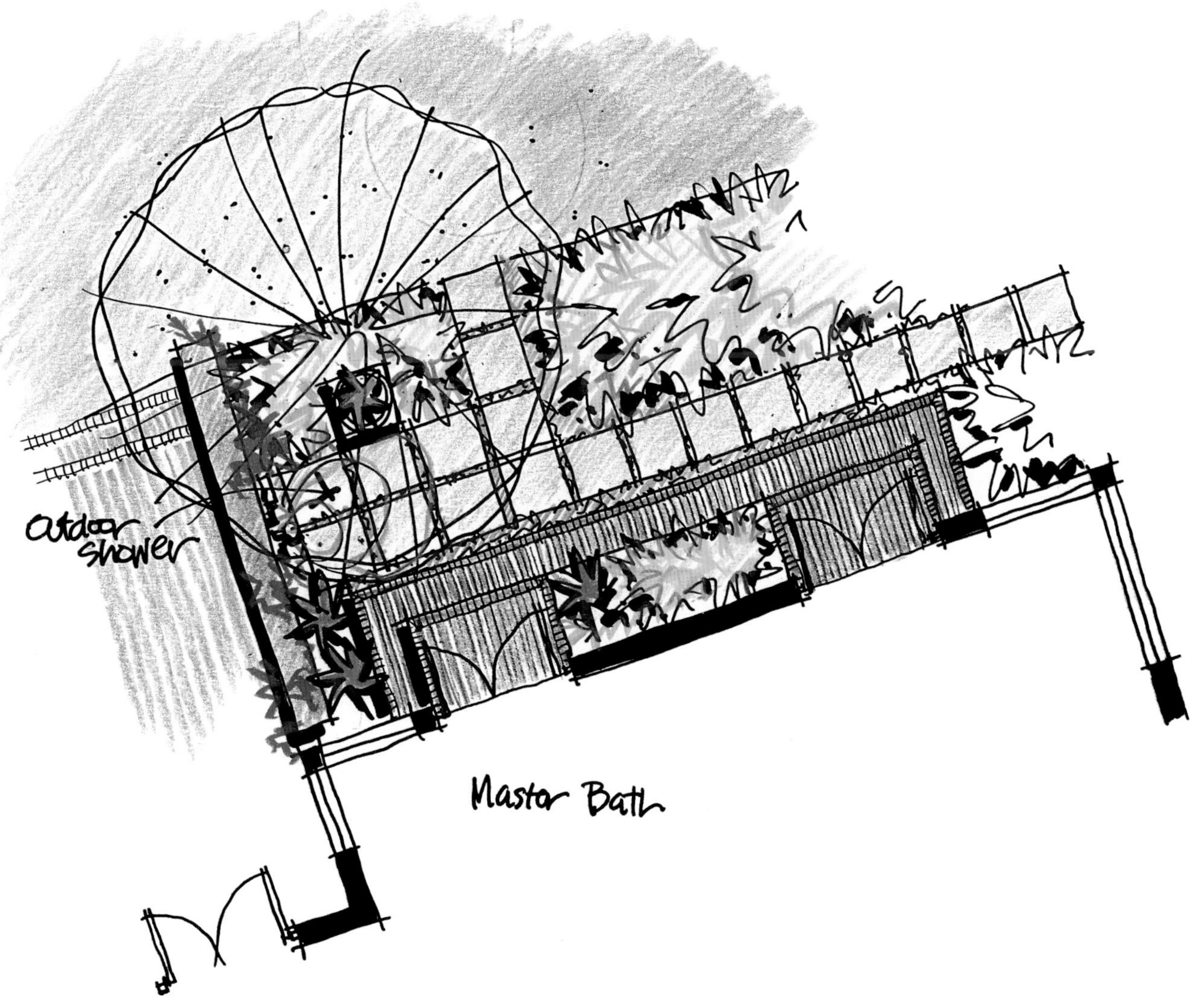
Outdoor shower
Master Bath

GROUND COVER

Mia Lehrer & Associates

"My garden is my laboratory," says landscape architect Mia Lehrer who, for the last 10 years has used her garden as a place to test ideas for clients. Approaching her property, all appearances suggest a traditional house and garden. Located on a steep hillside, the garden surrounds a 1920s bungalow; a white picket fence parallels the sidewalk. Upon opening the gate, the true nature of the garden reveals itself. Steps painted silver lead to a terrace of recycled green glass tumbled smooth enough to walk on barefooted. An immense 7-foot terra cotta vase sits on the hillside. Banks of ivy and a yellow flowering vine are espaliered on a vibrant purple stucco wall.

Other areas of this small garden are less avant garde, allowing the landscape architect to experiment with more conventional garden materials.

BIG IDEA: Mia Lehrer, known for her graphic, modernist gardens, has created an environment that is at once familiar and full of surprises. The beautifully detailed white picket fence surrounding the traditional bungalow recalls pleasant suburban communities from an earlier era. Yet the materials and colors used to design the garden as well as to decorate the house's interior are decidedly contemporary and urban

Above: A view down the silver entry stairs form the terrace covered with recycled green glass.

Right: The beautifully detailed white picket fence provides few clues as to what lies beyond.

Photography: Jay Venezia

2227

Right: The bold colors, large-scale pottery, and recycled glass ground cover contrast sharply with traditional plantings including *Bougainvillaea brasiliensis* Espalier.

GARDEN PLAN

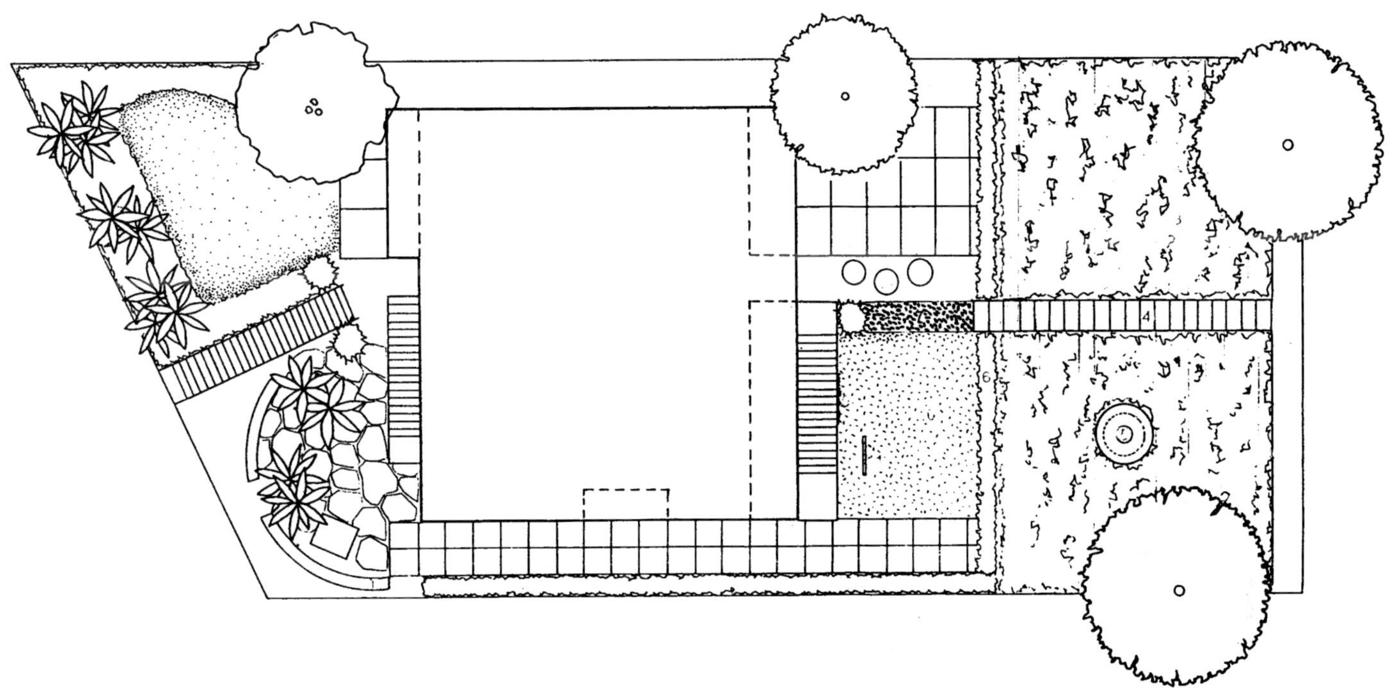

Left, clockwise from top: The silver entry steps; juxtaposition of smooth river stone and recycled glass; the stone entryway flanked by the recycled glass terrace; the gravel water basin as seen from above.

Left: Bougainvillaea 'weep' over the stacked concrete water wall fountain.

CONFINED SPACES

Dunn Hamelin Kane

Ten years after the landscape architects first worked on the gardens of this residence designed by the architecture firm of Gwathmey Siegel, they were asked to return to rework the design of the entry courtyard. Originally intended as a flat plane providing a base for the house and the parallel stone wall, the *Vinca minor* ground cover never filled in as hoped. The owners are avid gardeners and over time turned the courtyard into a flower and herb garden. Concern for accessibility to these ground-level gardens prompted them to request a new design that would address this problem while adding visual interest to the flat, open space.

BIG IDEA: The entry garden is a beautifully scaled space with a strong sense of enclosure. Columns spaced at 21-foot intervals expose the building's structural rhythm and divide the semi-enclosed loggia into four equal spaces. During the design process, the raised planters were considered as sculptural elements that added pattern and rhythm to the courtyard. This rhythm is complemented by the interplay between dark green lawn and gravel surface, imparting a Yin/Yang effect. The planters are 21-inches high with 24-inch wide caps for seating; their dimensions respect the architectural module of the house while providing easy access to the herbs and perennials growing in them.

Right: From the house, a view across the planters to the 42-inch high dry stacked stone retaining wall. A granite fountain is in the foreground. Its free-form shape contrasts with the strong geometry of the planters.

Photography: Charles Mayer

GARDEN PLAN

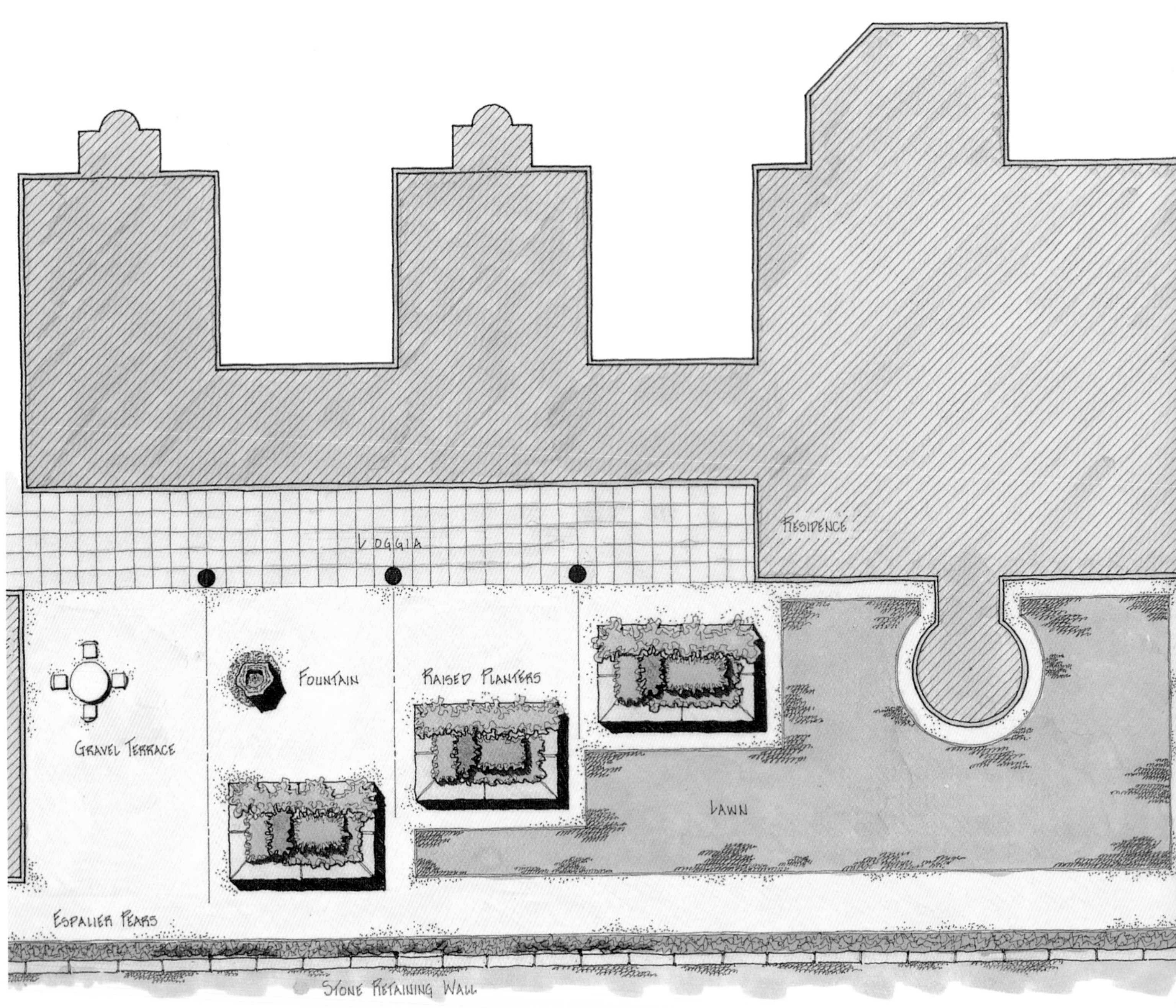

Residence
Loggia
Fountain
Raised Planters
Gravel Terrace
Lawn
Espalier Pears
Stone Retaining Wall

Right, top: A view of the retaining wall espaliered with *Pyrus* (pear).

Right: Herbs such as basil, lavender, rosemary, and thyme fill the planters along with perennials including astilbe, autumn joy sedum, Asian lily, and Siberian iris.

Left: The fountain creates a visual counterpoint within the courtyard.

Right: A view looking back toward the house and entry loggia.

ORCHARD GARDEN

Pamela Burton & Company

This garden at the landscape architect's own residence is sited within a cultivated grove of Valencia oranges. Conceptually, it examines the history of layers of cultivation within the wilderness. The Topa Topa Mountains at the perimeter of California's Ojai Valley where the property is located represents the first layer. The orange groves reference the second layer, and the final layer is represented by the 70-year-old stone house and garden enclosed by a series of stone walls.

The most popular space in the garden is under the grape arbor (planted in the 1930s by an Italian family who lived there).The thick vines not only produce an abundance of table grapes but also provide valuable shade from Ojai's hot summers. Roses are planted in profusion along the stone walls and a "Cecil Brunner" climbing rose dominates the front porch. The main entry from the orange grove to the house is anchored by a singular California pepper tree.

BIG IDEA:

To separate the garden from the orange grove, the landscape architect created what she terms a 'garden manifold'. "Like the huge thick cast iron part of a car engine, I separated the grove from the house with 2 1/2-foot thick dry mortar masonry walls." These walls extend those built by the previous owner. They are constructed of rocks from the surrounding mountains. Behind these walls, there are a series of interlocking triangles within the garden including meadow grasses, buffalo grass, and grama grass. All require minimal irrigation and no mowing.

Right: Pilasters adjoined by a stone bench separate the formal entry from the informal entry.

Photography: Pamela Burton.

Left: A bowl of oranges from the grove sits on the front porch.
Photograph: Tim Street-Porter

Right: Around the front porch, the climbing "Cecil Brunner" rose blooms profusely each spring.

GARDEN PLAN

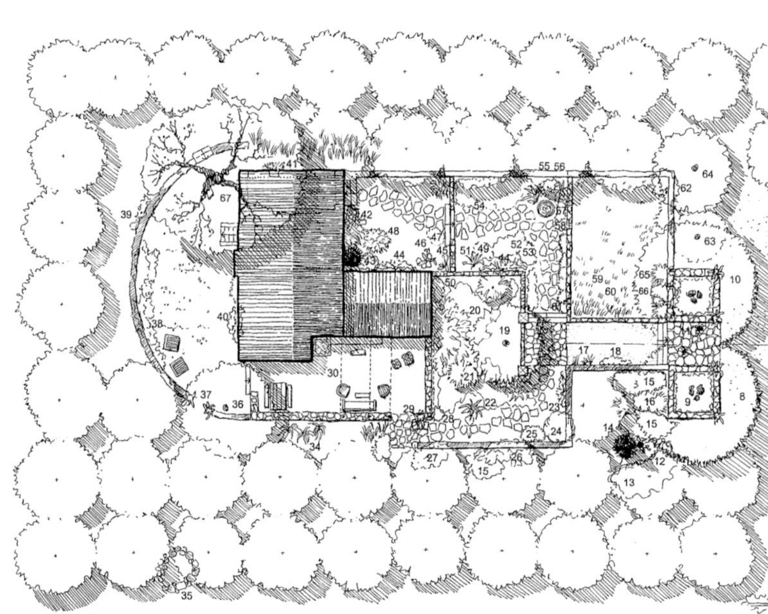

1 Citrus grove
2 Olea europaea
3 Ligustrum japonicum 'Texanum'
4 Acacia baileyana
5 Agave americana
6 Aloe arborescens
7 Lonicera japonica
8 Platanus acerifolia
9 Tulbaghia violace
10 Agave americana–terra cotta
11 Erigeron karvinskianus
12 Distictis buccinatoria
13 Duranta repens
14 Cupressus sempervirens
15 Phlomis purp 15 15
16 Buddleia davidii 'Black Knight'
17 Gaura lindheimeri
18 Bauhinia galpinii
19 Schinus molle
20 Acanthus mollis
21 Punica granatum
22 Agave tequilana
23 Rosa eglanteria
24 Lavatera maritima
25 Cistus 'Doris Hibberson'
26 Buddleia 'Pink Delight'
27 Rosa 'Mme Berkeley'
28 Dalechampia dioscoreifolia
29 Cuphea micropetala
30 Grape arbor
31 Iris douglasiana
32 Buddleia davidii 'Dark Knight'
33 Buddleia davidii 'Pink Delight'
34 Agave species
35 Nico's marshmello fire circle
36 Persimmon
37 Agave americana 'variegata'
38 Rosa
39 Rosa laevigata
40 Rosa 'Joseph's Coat'
41 Wisteria
42 Rosa 'Cecile Brunner'
43 Carpenteria californica
44 Rosa 'Gruss Au Achen'
45 Canna 'Intrigue'
46 Opuntia robusta
47 Verbena bonariensis
48 White Wisteria tree
49 Cistus ladanifer
50 Rosa 'Golden Showers'
51 Aloe thraskii
52 Lobelia laxiflora
53 Hesperaloe parviflora
54 Viola plectostachys
55 Agave attenuata 'Nova'
56 Rosa 'Rubrum'
57 Penstemon 'Midnight'
58 Crassula
59 Buchloe pactyloides
60 Bouteloua gracilis
61 Heliocototrichon sempervirens
62 Himalayan Musk Rose
63 Baer's Lime
64 Avocado
65 Echium fatuosum 'Select Blue'
66 Salvia verticillata
67 Jacaranda mimosifolia

Left: The "borrowed view" of the Topa Topa mountains.
Photograph: Tim Street-Porter

Right: A sketch of the garden and surrounding orchard.

Left: Low stone walls separate the garden from the surrounding orchard and enclose *Lavatera* and old fashioned *Acanthus.*

Right: A view of the orchard from the terrace.
Photograph: Tim Street-Porter

SOOTHING SPOT

Susan Raymond

The significant feature of this small courtyard garden is the water fountain. Its presence here has multiple meanings because the garden is located in the flood irrigation district of central Phoenix, Arizona. The fountain's shape is reminiscent of an irrigation standpipe, and it is designed to allow the water to spill gently over the sides. The water is left untreated so that wildlife can drink unharmed.

The garden is planted with seasonal native wildflowers including Penstemon, lupine, poppy, and Verbena. Hummingbirds, bees, and butterflies are attracted to plantings of cherry red sage, firewheel, 'Katie' ruellia, and coreopsis. The small Gregg Ash trees shade the courtyard's west walls. Deer grass graces the rear of the fountain and an Arizona sycamore was placed in the arc of the banco to provide additional shade. Its fragrance is similar to native streambeds.

Right: A concrete banco arcs around the courtyard and the fountain.

Below: A detail of the recycled concrete pavers.

Photography: Christopher Brown

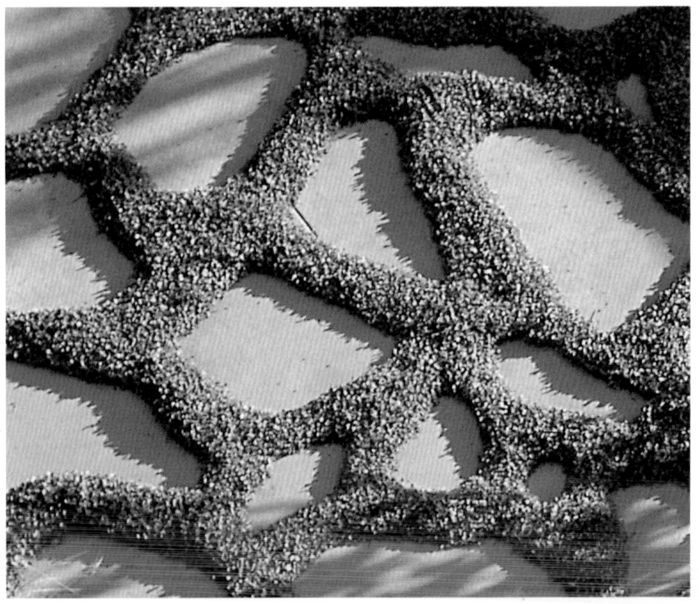

BIG IDEA: The paving stones in the garden are recycled from the front yard driveway which was jackhammered and replaced with less light reflective granite. Instead of transporting the pieces of concrete to a landfill, they were moved to the garden, and interplanted with dichondra, a low-growing groundcover. The driveway was 40 years old so the surface of the pavers appear to be sandblasted; this rough surface also makes them slip resistant.

GARDEN PLAN

Right: Deer grass is planted at the rear of the fountain and this form, 'Regal Mist', produces red-violet clouds in the fall.

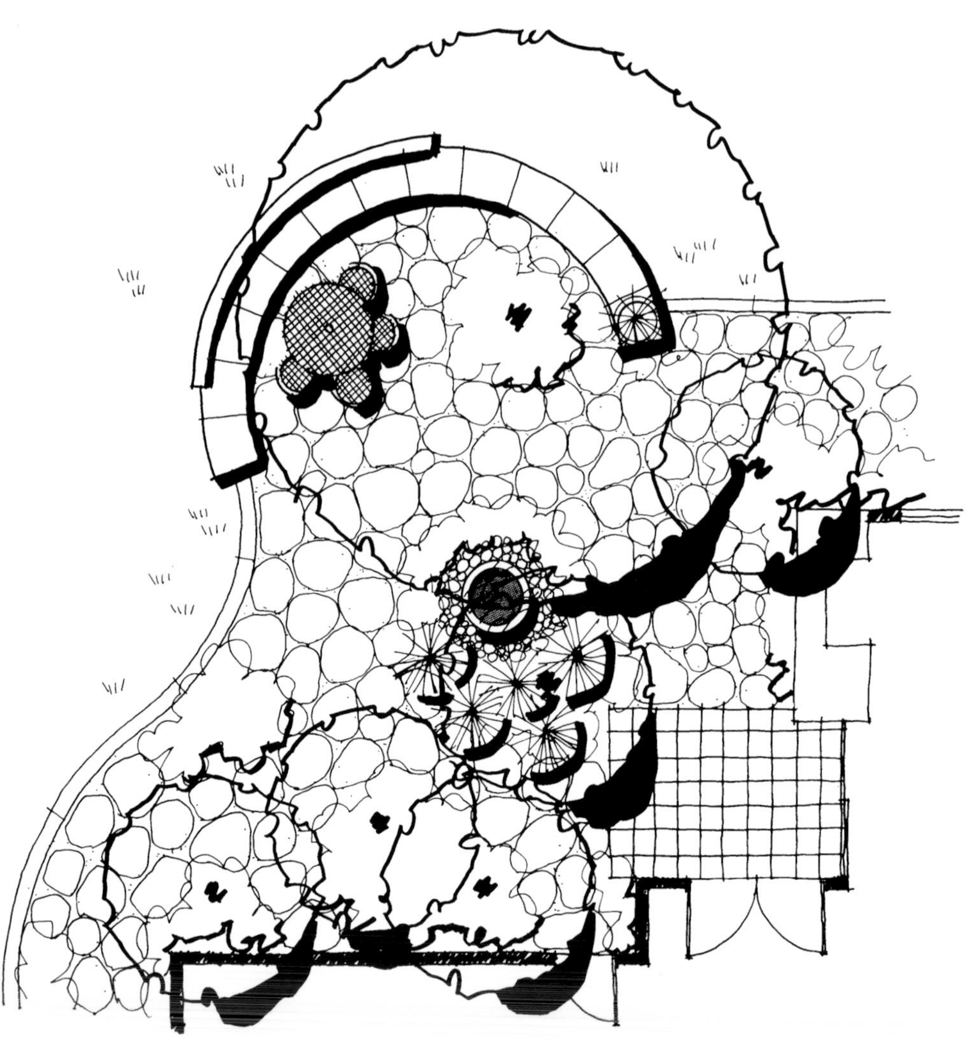

FOUNTAIN DREAMS

Oehme, van Sweden & Associates

This garden, located behind a townhouse in historic Georgetown in Washington, D.C., is prominently viewed from the family room. Because the garden is constantly on display, the owner wanted a variety of plant materials to create year-round seasonal interest. Large, overhanging flowering cherry, as well as neighboring trees restrict sunlight in the garden. Therefore, plants that thrive in the shade such as hosta, astilbe, and liriope were chosen. Many moisture-loving plants were placed near the fountain. Lush plantings also screen views of the rear garden areas while stepping stones draw the viewer into its depth. A small bluestone terrace with fieldstone and gravel features a counter with built-in cabinets for buffets. Uplights for trees and low-level lights for the garden around the terrace enliven plantings at night.

BIG IDEA:

A Japanese spirit effuses this garden. The use of different stone types with a dry stream of rock imbedded into the terrace evoke details from Japanese gardens. The custom-designed granite fountain with water spiraling from the top center out to its rim provides a focal point from the house and the terrace.

Right: The pink granite fountain is placed midway along a dry stream of stone.

Photography: James van Sweden

Left: A view of the garden from the patio.

Right: A detail of the dry stream of stone that meanders from the terrace to the rear of the garden.

GARDEN PLAN

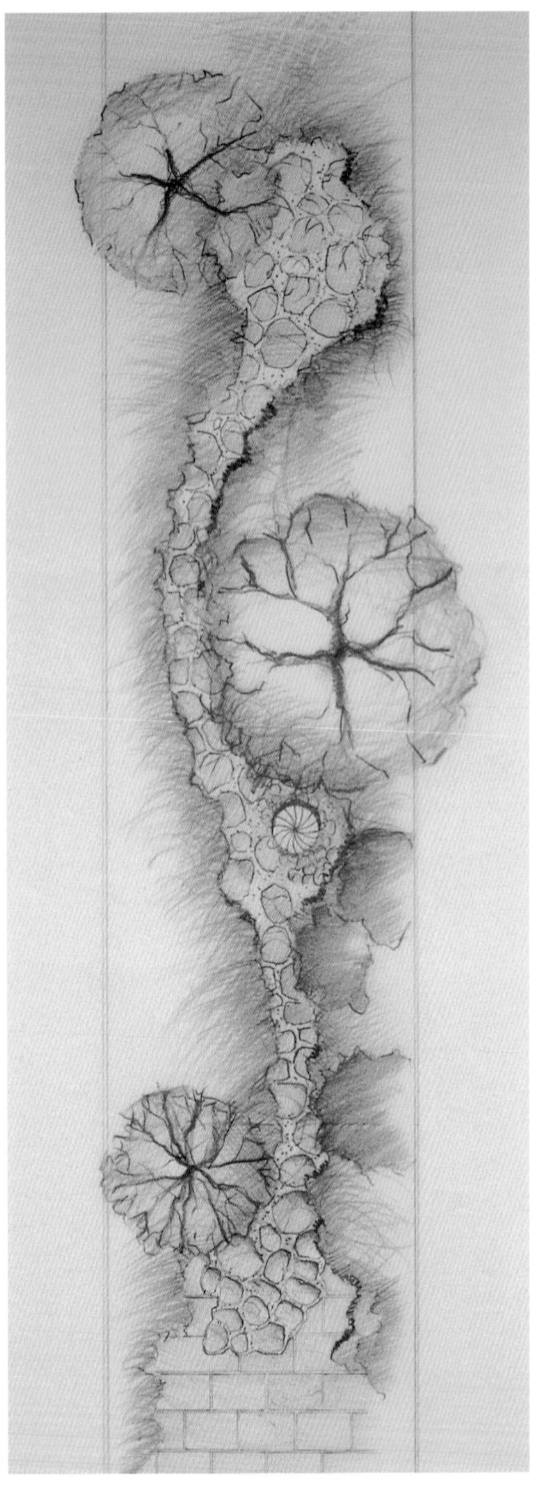

Right: A detail of the stone in autumn.

VILLA PISANO

Bunker Stimson Solien

BIG IDEA:
In order to accommodate the client's use-intensive program, the narrow sloping site was restructured with three terraces. These terraces provide the level expanses for vegetable and flower gardens, and recreation.

This project began with the renovation of a 19th century Greek revival farmhouse. The rear of the house was extended to accommodate a new kitchen and family room. The narrow, sloping lot required significant cutting and grading for the building addition.

The owners admire Italian hillside gardens, and had an extensive landscape program that included organic vegetable gardens, a perennial garden, fountain, terraces, a bocce ball court, and a croquet lawn. The design goal was to integrate elements of an Italian hillside landscape into a New England setting, where this property is located.

A working garden with raised stone-edged beds and stone and gravel terraces was sited adjacent to the house. A rich pavement palette of peastone, bluestone, and copper creates a strong graphic design. The middle level houses a bocce ball court, shaded by a grape arbor, overlooks the perennial and cutting beds as well as a fountain. Situated beyond the arbor, is a third terrace with a croquet lawn bordered by rose covered beach stone retaining walls.

Right: A view of the terraces. In the foreground is the bluestone terrace. The middle terrace is dominated by the arbor and beyond is lawn for croquet.

Photography: Eric A. Roth

Left: From the lawn, a view of garden toward the back of the renovated house. Particular attention to the design of the rear addition resulted in sweeping views of the garden.

Below: A close-up of the bocce balls.

GARDEN PLAN

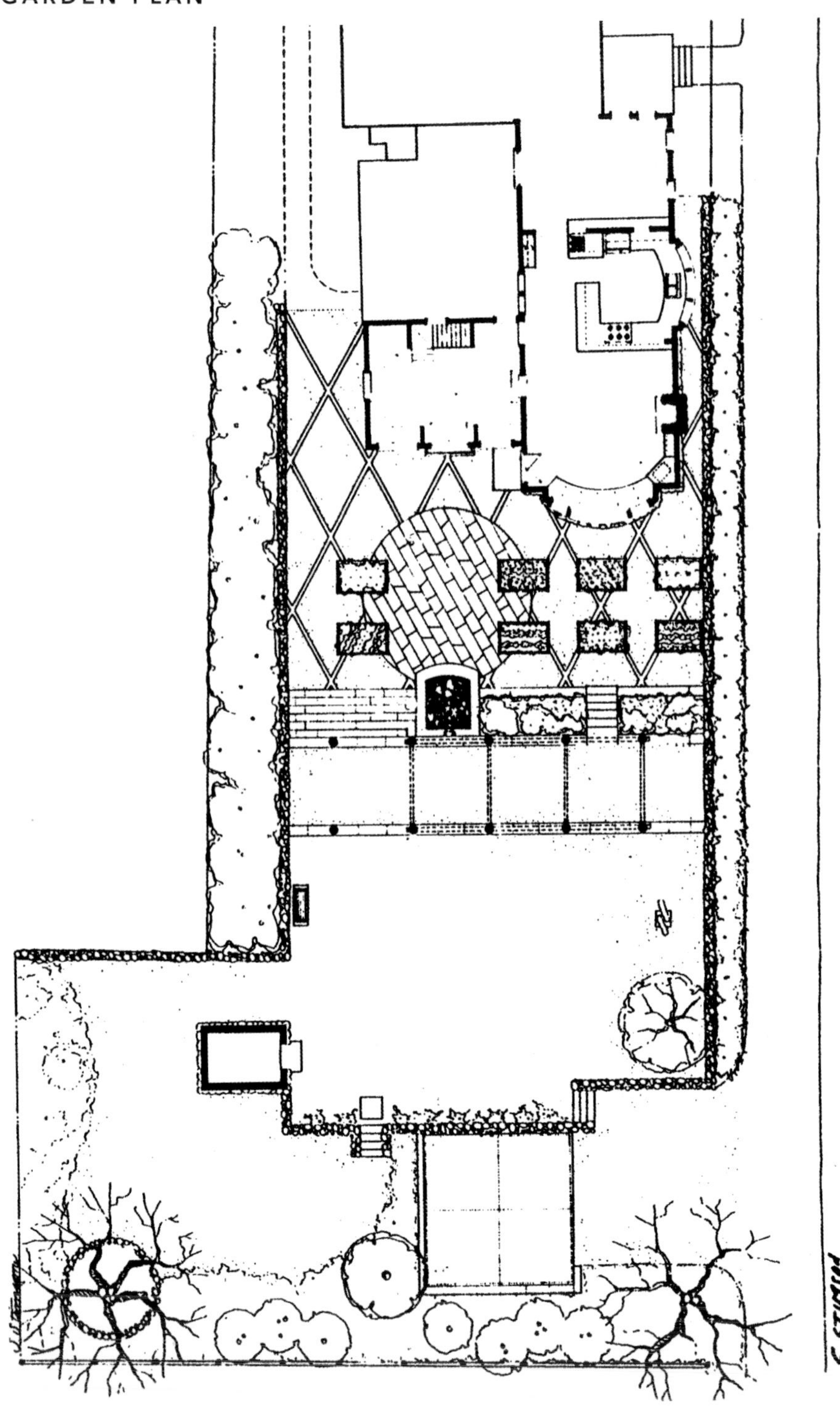

Right: A view of the arbor with yellow day lilies.

Left: Raised planters of kale, lettuce, and tomatoes are edged with vertical bluestone slabs bolted together.

HILLSIDE GARDEN

Dunn Hamelin Kane

This hillside garden includes a two-level terrace, a pool, and rock and perennial gardens. It is organized into two distinct zones. The dining terrace is connected to the kitchen and family room, providing a seating area and a comfortable transition to the outdoors. This terrace has a strong sense of enclosure. The lower garden's main feature is an undulating pool partially enclosed by low shrubs and perennials. The two zones are separated by a boulder wall rock garden connected by bluestone steps.

BIG IDEA: Creating a sense of enclosure is very important when designing intimate spaces. The degree of enclosure can be manipulated with a wide range of elements. Complete enclosure can be achieved with architectural elements such as a building, wall, fence, or hedge. Space can also be defined with transparent elements including low walls, shrubs, fences, or trees. All of these devices were employed here to create a garden with human scale that maintains short and long distance or "borrowed" views.

Right: Built into the boulder wall, the pool has a rugged quality–rough stone coping and boulders are placed at key locations.

Photography: Charles Mayer

GARDEN PLAN

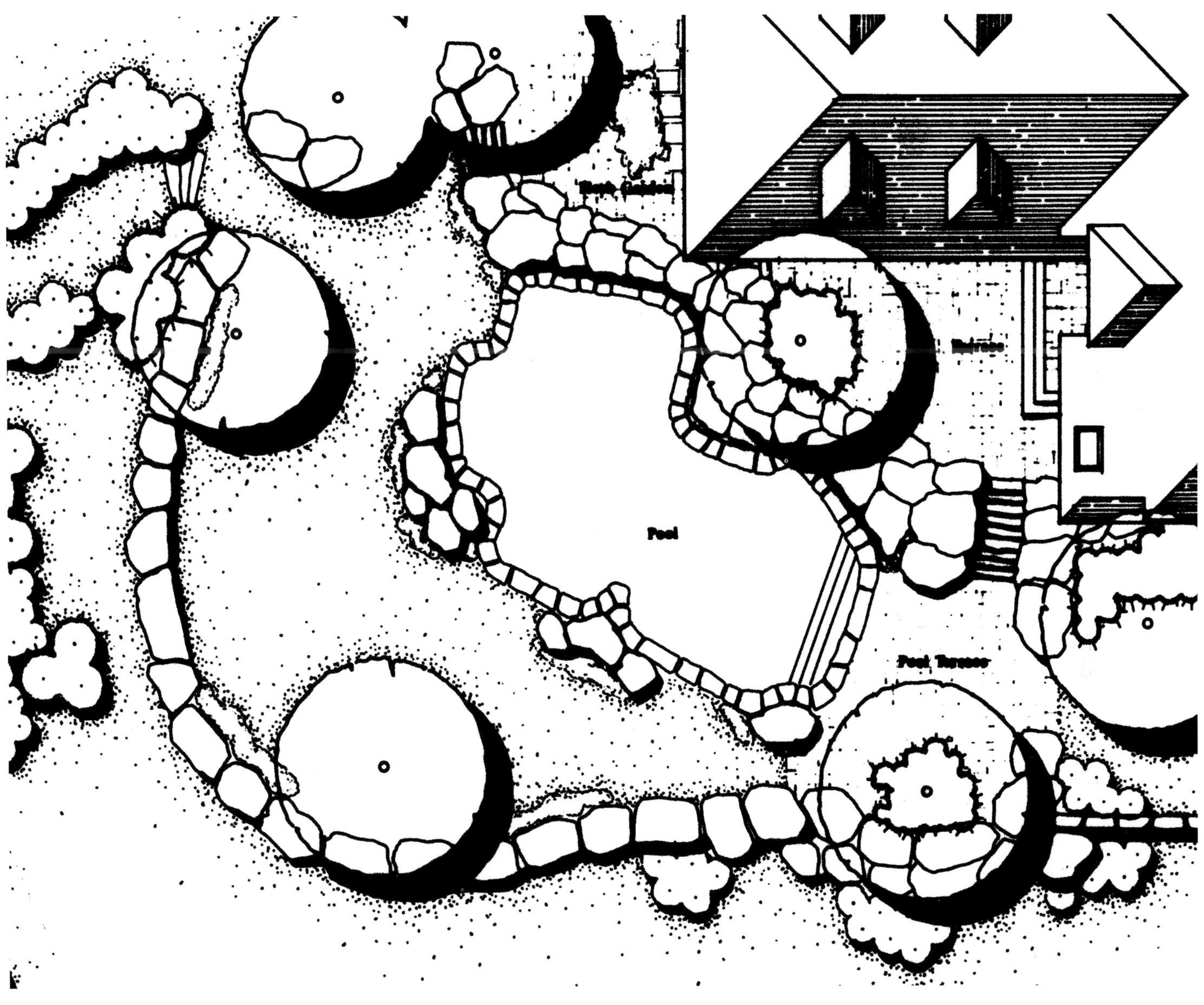

Left: The stone wall divides the upper terrace from the swimming pool.

Left: The small bluestone terrace connecting the upper and lower zones of the garden is also used for sunning and as a visual anchor for the pool.

Below: Peonies and irises adjacent to the pool.

Right: Junipers serve as a transition between the boulder structure and the garden.

Below: A detail of a twig trellis in the garden.

Right: A view across the pool to the terrace and the house.

PARALLEL PATHS

Samuel H. Williamson

When the current owners purchased this 1806 Federal row house located in crowded, busy Georgetown in Washington, D.C., the garden was overgrown with English ivy and weeds. Broken pottery was found when excavating the garden, calling to mind the utilitarian role of row house backyards in the 19th century.

In conjunction with an extensive restoration of the house, the landscape architect was asked to create a garden that would establish a dialogue with the Federalist architecture. The result is a spare, almost minimalist design that reflects the austere, democratic, anti-European aesthetic characteristic of Federal style. By contrast, the soft, green, shady plant palette provides a cool respite during Washington's hot summers.

BIG IDEA: Rather than divide the long, narrow garden into smaller rooms (a common design solution) the landscape architect chose a different tactic. His design reinforces the site's strongest characteristic–its depth. Parallel brick paths extend the full length of the garden from the rear of the house to a small, shady terrace at the far end. A narrow water runnel is framed by the paths and fed by a fountain that flows from stones at its terminus near the rear terrace. On the west side of the garden, and extending its length, is a row of six 'Heritage' river birch. Seven more of these graceful trees stand at the rear of the garden, behind the terrace.

Right: As seen from the dining room, parallel brick paths flanking the water runnel connect the house with the wooded terrace at the rear of the garden.

Photography: Roger Foley

GARDEN PLAN

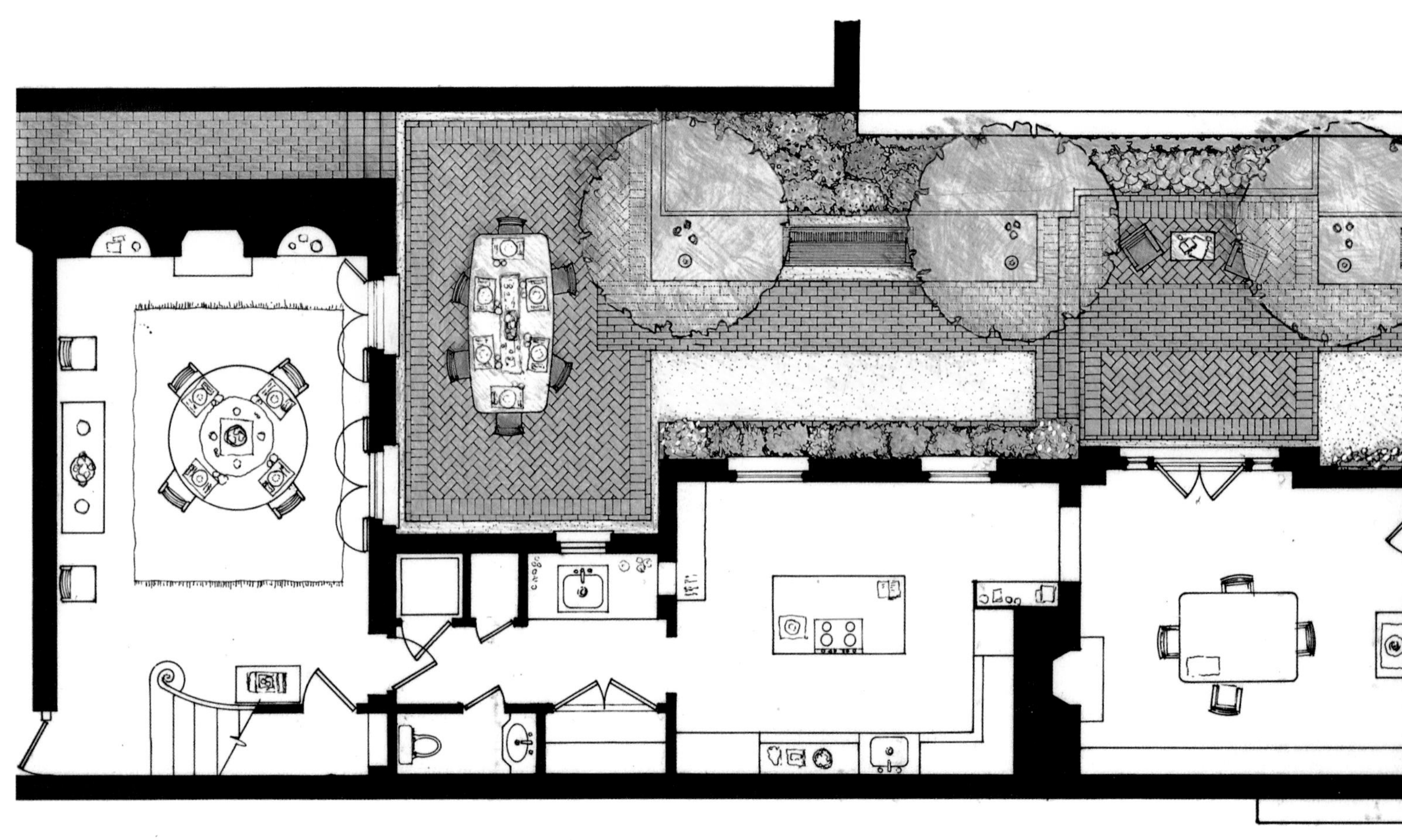

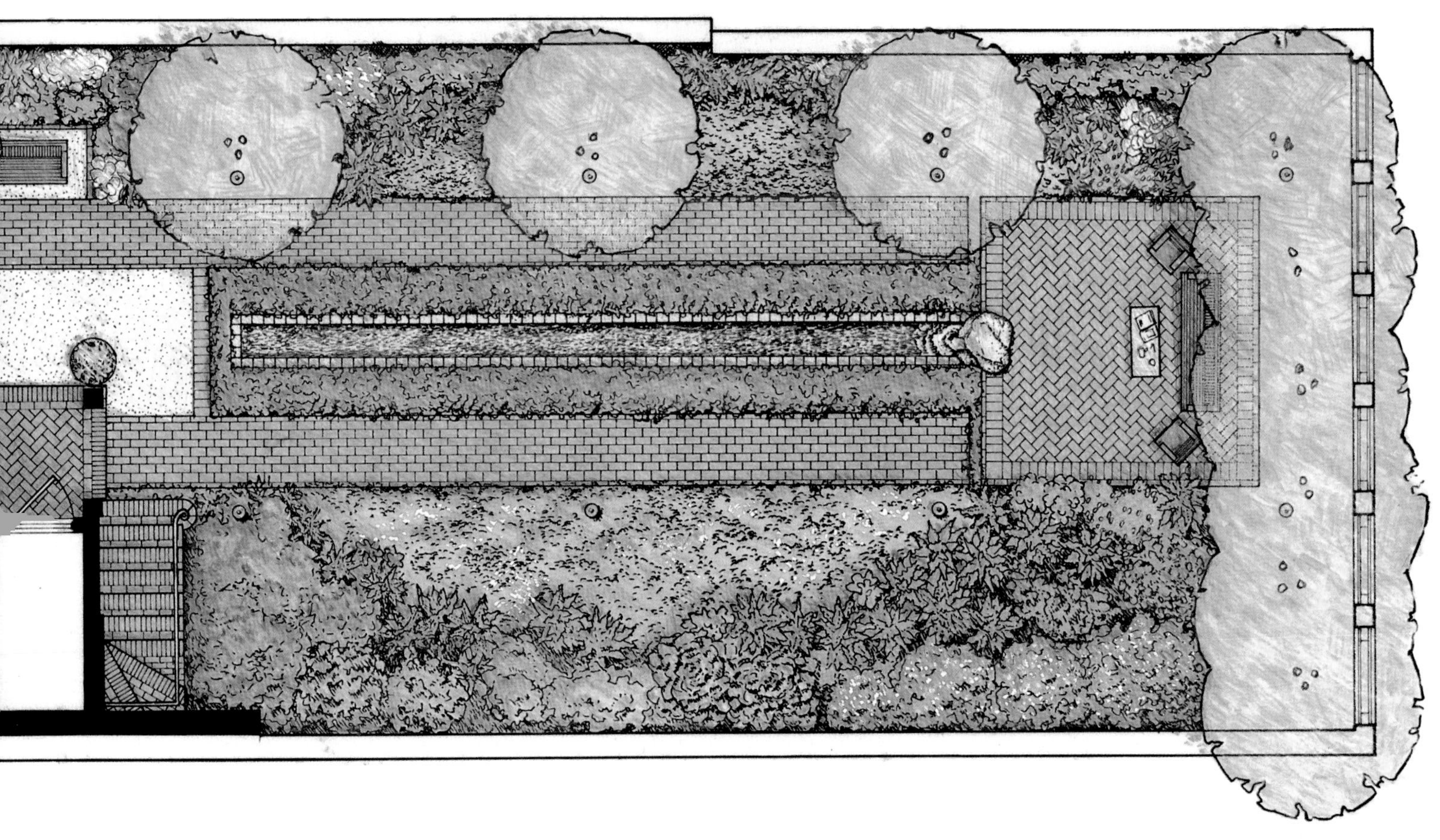

Above: The runnel is bordered with hosta, helix 'Needlepoint', and 'Green Gem' (two varieties of English ivy).

Right: View from the terrace looking back to the house.

DRAINAGE AS GARDEN ART

Joseph S. R. Volpe

This garden was created in conjunction with the restoration of a turn-of-the-century carriage house. The main house dominates the front of the one-quarter acre lot, while the three-story carriage house sits low, carved into the steep hillside at the rear. Extensive grading and retaining wall construction was necessary to take full advantage of the steep site. The landscape architect designed handsome stone drainage ways that safely redirect storm water from the street. The water is held in retention basins in the south stone terrace as well as the constructed wetland on the north side of the house. In spite of the garden's steep terrain and modest size, the small terraces around the carriage house connect to the garden stairs, walls, and tall trellises to create a strolling garden.

BIG IDEA: The ecology of drainage is integral to the design of this landscape. Directing the surface water from the street and front of the property down the steep slope at the rear was not just an engineering challenge but a design challenge as well. Surface water is redirected away from the house toward a southeasterly swale that is sculpted as a serpentine channel overlaid with smooth glacial stone. The swale leads to the south shingle terrace where the storm water is retained in a gravel cavity beneath the surface, providing irrigation for the maple trees before it continues its journey east to the drainage easement on the adjoining property.

Above: Detail of stairs to the lawn.

Right: The "postage stamp lawn" is only 12-by-15 feet square. It is edged by chunks of basalt laid slightly above grade and infilled with black anthracite coal.

Photography: Joseph S. R. Volpe

Left: The south shingle terrace off the main floor of the carriage house.

Above: The storm drainage waterway leading to the south terrace links dining and kitchen activities with the stroll garden. The landscape architect designed the drainage channel as a work of garden art.

GARDEN PLAN

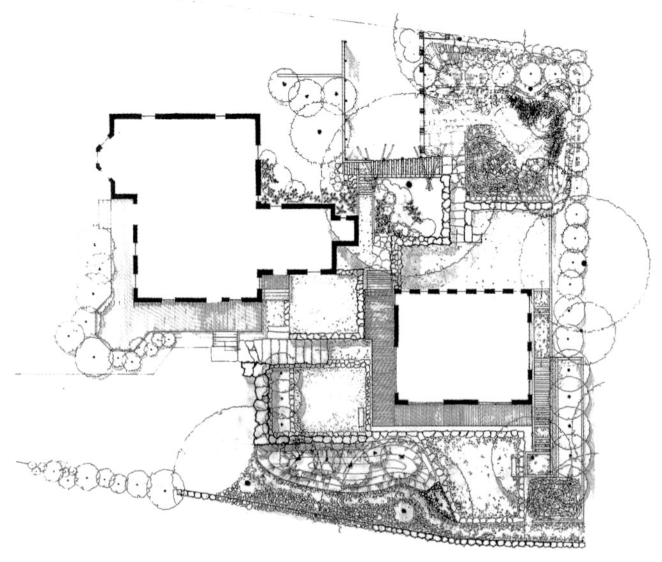

JOSEPH S.R. VOLPE, ASLA, PRINCIPAL PLANNER AND DESIGNER; SALVATORE M. VOLPE, ZEBEDEE J. VOLPE, MARCUS M. WILKES, ASSOICATES; SCOTT ALDRICH, CHUNG KIM, JOSEPH FICOCIELLO, IAN SCOTT RAMEY, ASSISTANTS.

SECTION

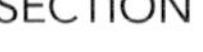

SECTION

DRAWINGS BY ZEBEDEE J. VOLPE

Far left: The deck along the carriage house connects the east and south terraces with the kitchen and dining rooms.

Left: The south terrace at the entrance; stairs lead to the the north wetlands garden.

Right: The red trellis on the north garden stairs screens the car parking area in the alley and leads down to the tiny wetland garden.

SOUTH-FACING TERRACE

Samuel H. Williamson

On the banks of the Charles River west of Boston, Massachusetts, the landscape architect was asked to create a series of small terraces that would afford views of the distant landscape. Along the northernmost end of the terrace, a bank of French doors open from the heart of the house. From point of origination, two limestone paths lead the visitor first into a cool, shady terrace, and then on to a larger, sunnier terrace. To the right, directly outside the dining room, is a small dining terrace. Between the paths, a small bubbling pool of water spills over a wall to a curving runnel that passes between white birches and, finally, over another lip to a lower pool.

BIG IDEA: Plantings were chosen to take advantage of the terraces' varied microclimates that progress from full shade to full sun. Lavender, thyme, and hardy grasses thrive in the sunny, mediterranean-like portions. Shaded areas are planted with azaleas, Irish moss, and mountain laurel and reference the New England woodlands.

Above: A detail of the water from the runnel spilling over the lower pool.

Right: From the pool in front of the french doors, the water spills into the runnel that parallels the limestone paths.

Photography: Adrian Catalano

GARDEN PLAN

Left: From the terrace, the distant landscape is in clear view.

Clockwise from top left: Beyond the terraces, chaise lounges designed by John Danzer of Munder Skiles appear as sculptures on the lawn; the dining terrace with furniture also by Danzer; detail of paving extending from the terrace onto the lawn.

Right: A view toward the French doors leading out to the shady terrace.

Left: The pool at the top of the runnel.

COURTYARD DINING

Floor & Associates, Inc.

For their own residence, the owners (both landscape architects) wanted to blur the lines between the interior and exterior spaces. Their home was extensively remodeled to include entire walls of single, light French doors that unite the interior, both visually and functionally with a series of separate, yet interconnected patios.

The north courtyard shown here, functions as a sitting and dining room connecting the kitchen and living room of the main house with the guest house. It is designed as a life-size checkerboard comprising 64 squares of alternating concrete pavers and patterned brick. The walls of the courtyard are formed on two sides by the buildings, on the third side by a dark purple stucco fountain wall, and on the fourth side by a hedgerow of flowering sage.

BIG IDEA: The brick areas of the patio are planted with low-growing dichondra. During the summer, it grows aggressively, covering the bricks and softening the edges of the concrete pavers. In the winter months, the bricks are exposed once again. Despite the thick growth of plantings, the brick provides ample support for tables and chairs.

Right: The courtyard connects the main house with the guest house. Photograph: Rick Raymond

Photography: Christopher Brown

GARDEN PLAN

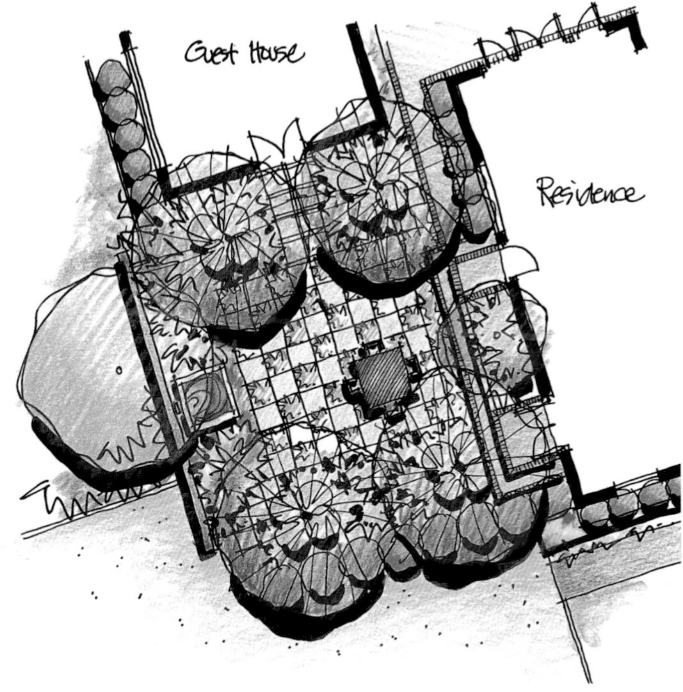

Left: The formal shape and orientation of the courtyard is accentuated by the small square pool centered on the stucco wall.

Right: The dark stucco wall is draped with a naval orange tree.

Right: In winter, the dichondra's growth slows, exposing the brick pattern underneath. Photograph: Rick Raymond

Far right: In the summer, the dichondra grows aggressively, covering the brick and softening the edges of the concrete pavers.

DESIGN DIRECTORY

Pamela Burton
Burton & Company
Santa Monica, CA

Andrew Cao
Landscape Architect
Los Angeles, CA

Dunn Hamelin Kane
Burlington, VT

Floor & Associates
Phoenix, AZ

Mario Schjetnan
Grupo de Diseño Urbano
Mexico, D.F.

Ron Herman
Landscape Architect
San Leandro, CA

Raymond Jungles
Landscape Architect
Key West, FL

Sheela Lampietti
Lampietti/Gardens Inc
Purcellville, VA

Mia Lehrer & Associates
Los Angeles, CA

Oehme, van Sweden & Associates
Washington, DC

Ken Smith
Landscape Architect
New York, NY

Stephen Stimson Associates
Falmouth, MA

Michael Van Valkenburgh Associates
Cambridge, MA

Joe Volpe, ASLA
Amherst, MA

Charles Warren Architect
New York, NY

Phillip Metcalf
Washington Water Gardens
McLean, VA

Samuel H. Williamson Associates
Portland, OR